Fellowship, Freedom
and Equality

FELLOWSHIP, FREEDOM AND EQUALITY

Lectures in memory of R. H. Tawney

edited by
David Ormrod

CHRISTIAN SOCIALIST MOVEMENT

Published in 1990 by the
CHRISTIAN SOCIALIST MOVEMENT
47 Fyfield Road, London E17 3RE
Trade distribution by
CENTRAL BOOKS LTD
14 The Leathermarket, London SE1 3ER

British Library Cataloguing in Publication Data
Fellowship, Freedom and Equality : Lectures in memory of R. H. Tawney.
  1. Christian socialism
  I. Tawney, R. H. (Richard Henry) *1880–1962* II. Ormrod,
  David *1945-* III. Christian Socialist Movement
  335.7

ISBN 0-900286-01-6

Printed by Cox & Wyman Ltd, Cardiff Road, Reading, Berks RG1 8EX
Cover designed by Ruth Murray.

Acknowledgements

The Christian Socialist Movement is grateful to the lecturers for permission to reproduce their work. Lectures 1 to 9 inclusive have appeared before in pamphlet form; lecture 10 is printed here for the first time. An extended version of lecture 5 has appeared in Kenneth Leech, *Struggle in Babylon*, Sheldon, 1988. The Vicky cartoon of Tawney is reproduced by permission of the *New Statesman and Society*. The rose design on the front cover is reproduced by permission of the Labour Party to which CSM is affiliated.

The Christian Socialist Movement gratefully acknowledges support from The Christendom Trust and from individual members of CSM who have contributed in various ways to the publication of this book.

CONTENTS

David Ormrod
Introduction

R. H. Tawney, Socialist Prophet, 1880–1962

The 1980s in Britain saw the elevation of unscrupulous greed, inequality and self-interest to the status of a high moral creed. Intermittent opposition from the churches to the new idolatory of wealth surfaced from time to time but no individual critics have arisen with a combination of political wisdom, historical insight and moral force to match that of R. H. Tawney, the prophet who denounced acquisitiveness. Tawney's was undoubtedly the most forceful and authentic voice of Christian socialist prophecy to be raised during the 1920s and 30s, echoing into the 1950s.

Like Charles Gore, Tawney believed in the practical possibility of creating a just society based on the principles of the Sermon on the Mount — a vision and a goal which many Christian socialists have shared. Indeed, as Donald Soper has written, that hope 'runs like a golden thread through the whole of Christian life, history and tradition'. It is as vital and relevant to the 1990s as it was for the interwar years. So what was the special quality of Tawney's genius?

Tawney was not a great speaker and always, as he said, 'wrote out the whole damned thing'. William Temple and Stafford Cripps were much more effective speakers whose enormous meetings for the Industrial Christian Fellowship could fill the Albert Hall. In fact Tawney's influence came chiefly through his books, especially *The Acquisitive Society* (1921) and *Equality* (1931), which argued that a society based on unbridled self-interest, a society which makes the individual the centre of his or her own universe, 'creates its own nemesis, a malaise within itself which it has no power to cure'.

The effect was to 'conscientise' a whole generation in the 1920s and 30s, and this was coupled with a more concentrated influence within the Labour Party. He drafted its election manifestos in 1928 and 1934 as well as several policy documents of the 1930s but eschewed personal political ambitions and honours. He associated with groups and movements but did not become submerged by them. When president of the Socialist Christian League from 1947 onwards he played only a minor role in its activities, but contributed a stream of arcticles to the *Manchester Guardian, New Statesman* and other journals on politicial, educational and religious topics which only petered out in the last 10 years of his life. He presided at the foundation meeting of the modern Christian Socialist Movement in 1960.

Tawney's genius therefore lay in the special quality of his writing which captured and laid bare present reality as a continuum of definite historical changes. He realised, in other words, that 'what is supposed to be the past is in reality the present' — that realisation which forms the basis of true prophecy. Combined with this was an abundance of critical expertise. He was a professional historian of exceptional competence who, as one of his colleagues put it, 'above all else was a Christian, and what interested him was why an upper class which claimed to be Christian could have allowed history to take the way that it did'. This was the central theme of *Religion and the Rise of Capitalism* (1926) which attempted to describe and explain the inexplicable: the retreat of the Christian social tradition during the English Reformation.

Religion has rarely acted as a neutral force in society and Christianity especially has shown a remarkable capacity to adapt itself to changing economic and political circumstances, often in the interests of the privileged, whether feudal lords or capitalists. As Tawney pointed out, 'all creeds suffer at the hands of history a double deformation. They undergo a process of dilution and petrifaction — dilution by the world, petrifaction by the elect'. His strongest words were reserved for the Anglican Church which, he felt '. . . remains a class institution, making respectful salaams to property and gentility, and with too little faith in its own creed to call a spade a spade in the vulgar manner of the New Testament.'

Many have testified that Tawney was a brilliant teacher, but his research and writing were undertaken not simply to fulfil the obligations of a demanding academic career or to meet the needs of his students, important though these were. Unsurprisingly, as a protestant, he regarded history as a means of exploring fundamental truths, a material from which knowledge of human experience and destiny might be obtained. 'History is a maze', he wrote, 'all of whose windings are connected. Whatever the gate by which first they enter it, students who follow them through to the end may feel reasonably confident of approaching nearer the centre.'

It was from seventeenth-century English history that Tawney took his political bearings, and in his ambivalent love-hate relationship with English puritanism ('the schoolmaster of the bourgeoisie') we can see the historical reflection of his involvement with Christian socialism and the Labour Party. According to Richard Crossman, Tawney viewed the Labour Party as a Cromwellian new model army and in the 1930s, when a Labour government had been tried and had failed, changed his position. Crossman wrote, in 1960, 'He became not the visionary preacher of Christian socialism but a fierce Micah, castigating the chosen people for their shortcomings and prophesying doom unless their leaders repented. Will the stern advice he gave to a party torn and distracted by the 1931 fiasco assist us in our present factional disputes?' It was in 1934 that Tawney wrote '. . . the puritans, though unpleasant people, had one trifling merit. They did the job, or, at any rate, their job. Is the Labour Party doing it?'

As the depression deepened and the fascist menace spread, Tawney retained his loyalty to the Labour Party and although he became increasingly critical of its policies showed no sympathy for the Communist Party, as did many of his contemporaries. In his role as mentor to the Labour Party, Tawney had reached the political limits of his Christian socialism and felt no compulsion to extend this into Marxism. When, under the pressure of world events, the beginnings of Christian-

Marxist dialogue first stirred in Britain in 1935, Tawney played no part, although be believed that, 'The crisis of Europe today has some resemblance to that of three centuries ago'. It was John Macmurray, a communist sympathiser and a Congregationalist who laid the real foundations of Christian-Marxist dialogue together with John Lewis, Joseph Needham, Kenneth Ingram and others. Tawney steered a middle course between the Marxist-inclined Christian left and the earlier idealistic Christian socialism of the 1920s.

The Tawney Memorial Lectures, 1962–1989

For Christians and socialists today, Tawney's ideas possess a strength and resilience sufficient to provide the starting point and the inspriation for a variety of approaches within a framework which might be described as that of 'ethical socialism'. The lectures reprinted here testify to this diversity: their authors, for example, may occupy quite different positions within the Labour Party or outside it. Some have drawn substantially on Marxism while others would prefer to derive their socialism from Christian or other non-Marxist sources; some are highly critical of the church, others less so.

The Tawney memorial lectures are sponsored by the Christian Socialist Movement, and it is the purpose of this collection to make them available to a wider audience. The lectures are printed here in the order in which they were delivered, and hence provide a conspectus and a comparison of Christian socialist thinking in and between two periods: the 1960s, with lectures by **Stanley Evans** and **Charles Coulson** which, together with **Donald Soper's** more recent contribution, provide points of contact with Tawney's earlier generation; and the younger authors of the 1980s responding in a variety of ways to the tensions and pressures of the Thatcher decade.

Opening the second group of lectures, **Frank Field** signalled the end of post-war consensus politics and the rise in unemployment and poverty of the early 1980s. He outlined a programme for the radical redistribution of income to the poorer sections of society by reforming the tax benefit system. Field's worst expectations were of course realised as unemployment rose to a peak figure of 3.5 million in 1983–84. Social dislocation produced serious riots in 1981, and **Kenneth Leech's** lecture noted that the atmosphere created by Reagan and Thatcher, 'while it avoids the crudities of the fanatical racist groups, provides the ideological air in which they can breathe'. However, Leech went on to suggest that the recent history of black immigration reflected no credit on the Labour movement, and reminds us of the negative approach of the early Fabians to the issues of race and colonial development. Tawney had little to say about these questions, and the global dynamics of capitalism in the twentieth century were of less interest to him than its seventeeth century origins in north-western Europe.

For socialists in the 1980s, however, development issues became a major pre-occupation and this large area, together with the theology and political economy of liberation, form the underlying themes of the lectures by Irene Brennan, Cedric Mayson and Charles Elliott. **Irene Brennan** draws out the contrast between the European Christian-Marxist dialogues of the 1960s and the more recent synthesis of the Gospel and Marxism found in the liberation theologies of Latin America, the Philippines and parts of Africa and Asia. Here, the struggle for justice and liberation has given birth to a new praxis, replacing the old political and religious dogmas. Here, as **Cedric Mayson** describes it (and with particular reference to South Africa), we can witness the emergence of a 'liberated theological zone' in which 'God is no longer made in the image of the Emperor Constantine' but identifies himself with all people in a spirit of solidarity and compassion. As Gustavo Gutierrez emphasised, economic and political liberation necessarily go hand in hand with the liberation of a dependent church, and of theology itself. **Charles Elliott** concentrates primarily on the ideas of third-world economists but, in place of the familiar British-north American tendency to tell the developing countries where they are getting it wrong, applies their ideas to provide a critique of monetarist and other Thatcherite economic solutions to our own domestic problems.

The two final lectures by **Tony Benn** and **Pauline Webb** are concerned more directly with the moral basis for social action: in socialist politics, in the media and the vocabulary of political discourse. For each of these authors, the old debate about the balance between freedom and responsibility takes on a new significance in Britain at the end of a decade when genuine as distinct from formal freedoms have been relentlessly eroded. The priority for Christian socialists today, as Tony Benn suggests, is 'how to unite the ideas associated with fellowship and collective effort with freedom, to make it real in a pluralistic society where equality does not mean uniformity or meritocracy but makes it possible for us to be ourselves within the human family'.

Stanley Evans
Equality

From the publication of his *The Agrarian Problem in the Sixteenth Century* in 1912 to his *Business and Politics Under James I* in 1958, inadequate as it was as a biography of Lionel Cranfield, Richard Henry Tawney was an economic historian of the first rank: from the publication in 1915 of *The Establishment of Minimum Rates in the Tailoring Industry Under the Trade Boards Act of 1909* to *The Problem of the Public Schools* in 1943, he made a distinguished contribution to practical economics: as an educationalist his work ranged from his insistence in 1914 on the feeding of school children, through a major part in a League of Nations Report in 1932 on *The Reorganisation of Education in China* to a long presidency of the Workers' Educational Association: his quality as a political theorist can be studied in works which range from his 1919 introduction to Max Beer's *A History of British Socialism*, through his 1941 Lecture on *Harrington's Interpretation of His Age*, to the essays published in *The Attack, and other Papers* in 1953. In all this, and in a whole series of books and pamphlets and lectures that went with it, there was enough to make the reputations of several men. But the truth is that when you have considered it all you have not begun to think of the work which will constitute Tawney's abiding claim to fame. It was given to him to write three books each of which gave birth to a whole approach to a subject and which has influenced thought upon it ever since and each of these three works is based upon the application of a genuinely Christian morality to the detailed work of history, economics or politics. The books were *The Sickness of an Acquisitive Society* in 1920; *Religion and the Rise of Capitalism* in 1926 and *Equality* in 1931. In the first of these works he condemned the Acquisitive Society in which we live on grounds which were unanswerable: that it creates its own nemesis, a malaise within itself which it has no power to cure, and the many works which are now loose among us, about *The Stagnant Society* and *The Status Seekers* and many similar variations upon the same theme, do but reflect the profundity of his prophecy.

The second of these books has been followed by many other writers in the same field, but for all that it continues to stand alone: 'Societies,' said Tawney in his conclusion, 'like individuals have their moral crises and their spritual revolutions. The student can observe the results which these cataclysms produce, but he can hardly without presumption attempt to appraise them, for it is at the fire which they kindled that his own small taper has been lit. The rise of a naturalistic science of society, with all its magnificent promise of fruitful action and of intellectual light; the abdication of the Christian churches from departments of economic conduct and social theory long claimed as their province; the general acceptance by thinkers of a scale of ethical values which turned the desire for pecuniary gain from a perilous, if

Equality

natural, frailty into the idol of philosphers and the mainspring of society — such movements are written large over the history of the tempestuous age which lies between the Reformation and the full light of the eighteenth century. Their consequences have been worked into the very tissue of modern civilisation. Posterity still stands too near their source to discern the ocean into which these streams will flow.'

These words were written more than 40 years ago: 40 years in which in many ways the pace of certain modern developments has become ever more frantic. We are the generation that tosses in terror and all too often without hope upon the ocean which Tawney saw ahead; for us the waves rise and around us the winds shriek and there can be no survival unless a proper course is set and our frail bark is correctly trimmed and adequately handled. It is at this point that the greatness of Tawney emerges because it is in the third of the books to which I have referred, his *Equality*, that a beginning may be found of any basic thought adequate to the situation which we are in.

Equality was published in 1931 and was the substance of the Halley Stewart lectures for 1924. New editions were published in 1938 and 1951 and a Spanish edition in Mexico in 1945. It came from the years of mass unemployment and the first Labour government. What it asserted was to be found essentially in one paragraph: A nation will 'reflect that it is possible that, by attemtping to free its social life from traits, which possess, no doubt, an historical explanation, but which everyone knows in their heart to be repulsive and humiliating, it may also be fostering the temper which would enable it to mobilise more effectively its material resources, and to find some compensation in good will and intelligence for the adventitious advantages which history, and the set of the economic tide, and the movement of affairs in the world at large, once bore to its feet, but now bears no longer.' [1].

In Britain, said Tawney, the religion of inequality was observed 'on the scale of a national institution' and he quoted Matthew Arnold as having 'observed that in England inequality is almost a religion, and remarked on the incompatibility of that attitude with the spirit of humanity, and sense of the dignity of people as people, which are the marks of a truly civilised society.' He observed that a community 'requires a common culture and that without it it is not a community at all.' [2] But he insisted that 'to criticise inequality and desire equality is not, as is sometimes suggested, to cherish the romantic illusion that people are equal in character and intelligence. It is to hold that, while their natural endowments differ profoundly, it is the mark of a civilised society to aim at eliminating such inequalities as have their source, not in individual differences, but in its own organisation, and that individual differences which are a source of social energy, are more likely to ripen and find expression if social inequalities are, as far as practicable, diminished.' [3] His strategy of equality was based largely upon the redistribution of wealth and in this process he saw an expanding significance in all kinds of communal provision and the extension of social services, while he saw as the lion threatening the path of progress the system of the ownership of wealth which is the dominant factor of our society. But this, he held, could be changed. 'People have given one stamp to their institutions; they can give another. They have idealised money power; they can choose equality.' He finished by emphasising the danger to humanity of what our Elizabethan Bible, following the Greek, called 'mammon': 'In the currency of the soul,' he said, 'as in that of states, spurious coin drives out good. . . . The chief enemy of the life of the spirit . . . is the idolatry of wealth.'[4]

Whenever the question of equality is discussed the same objection is raised: 'we are not the same: people are made unequal.' On this it is assumed that the discussion is finished and generally speaking it is because we have been moulded by the subservient society and although we no longer touch our forelocks we have been trained from our earliest years in the appropriate methods of kow-towing to the right persons and few of us would have it otherwise. The real discussion never even begins because of a failure in semantics. It is not true that the word 'equal' has an identity of meaning with the word 'same' and the assumption that it does vitiates the entire discussion. The Latin word 'aequalis' from which we derive our word 'equal' means level, even, just; it is a word concerned with the relationship between one thing and another. The verb 'aequo' means to make level, even, smooth: the word even had a primary gambling connotation and 'aequare sortes' meant to see that the lots are equal in number to those who draw; 'aequalis' really meant our much abused word 'contemporary,' 'that can be compared in respect of the same age'. The word is again used of the evenness of the sea and Tacitus uses it precisely in our sense of political equality. There would be no need of a word 'equality' if, when we asserted the need of it, we were asserting the similarity of all or the identity of all. The concept of equality has, indeed, no meaning at all apart from a concept of relationships between those who are different and what it asserts is that however different they are they must accept a status the one with the other which is rooted in a common humanity. While one section of any community is inferior to another its growth and development is stunted and starved while the growth of the superior group is necessarily perverted. The loss to humanity as a whole which springs from inequality is immense because humanity has need, and dire need, of all that the human mind, all that human ingenuity, all that the human spirit, can produce. Anything which inhibits its growth is an evil disease which must be eradicated. Inequality is such a disease.

When Tawney wrote his famous book he was concerned with what he called 'the religion of inequality' in one country: we have to be concerned first of all with the fact of inequality in the world at large.

There is no political document in world history which speaks more strongly of equality than the Charter of the United Nations: 'We the peoples of the United Nations determined to save succeeding generations from the scourge of war, which twice in our lifetime has brought untold sorrow to mankind, and to reaffirm faith in fundamental human rights, in the dignity and worth of the human person, in the equal rights of men and women and of nations large and small, and to establish conditions under which justice and respect for the obligations arising from treaties and other sources of international law can be maintained, and to promote social progress and better standards of life in larger freedom, and for these ends to practise tolerance and live together in peace with one another as good neighbours, and to unite our strength to maintain international peace and security, and to ensure, by the acceptance of principles and the institution of methods, that armed force shall not be used save in the common interest, and to employ international machinery for the promotion of the economic and social advancement of all peoples, have resolved to continue our efforts to accomplish these aims.'

The words are as fresh today as when they were first penned. Then they interpreted effectively the social aspirations of millions of people slowly and arduously emerging from the long-drawn sufferings of the most cataclysmic war of human history: they are words which may have sounded natural on the lips of a Roosevelt, but never did they seem the natural modes of expression of Messrs Churchill, Stalin and De Gaulle. Today they sound bizarre. How can there be tolerance between absolute righteousness and Belial, between east and west or west and east? And yet when first published these words were jointly signed between capitalist and communist representatives and the idea they enshrined, that peoples were sovereign, not one more than another, but sovereign in equality, and had a right to their own social systems which they alone might change, was an eminently sensible idea to which we shall still have to return. The political philosophy of this declaration is, indeed, as staggering as it is prophetic. It does not begin with 'We, the leaders' or 'We, the government' but 'We, the peoples'. It asserts the most profound equality of all, the right of peoples to govern themselves and in so doing to stand together with all other peoples. This was not a fact at the time; it is a principle which has been denied and blasphemed since 1945 in every dependent colonial territory; in one sovereign state after another; in crises from Korea to Cuba. Its achievement will, in very truth, be the revolution, but without it people will not be human, political democracy will be but a phrase, and peace will not be secure. Faith was reaffirmed in fundamental human rights and the dignity and worth of the human person and in the equal rights of men and women and of nations large and small. The concept of inalienable human rights, of rights which spring from the fact of human nature, an expression of the ancient theory of a natural law which may not be overthrown, a standing rejection of the idea that a state can do what it likes and its people must obey, is the basis of all equality: it is a notion which few governments really like and it has been assailed in the most savage ways in recent years. Angola and the Union of South Africa are but two states which have demonstrated that when this theory is denied, barbaric cruelty follows. Equal rights of men and women are still far from achievement and, in the light of contemporary practice, to talk of the equal rights of nations large and small seems remote indeed. Diplomatic practice concedes no such equality; an ambassador is sent to an important country, to a less important country a minister, and so on through a descending scale; the protocol is related to the practice and the measure of equality that is conceded relates more to the strength of armament that is carried than to anything else. If it were Stalin who asked in the war, when something was said of the views of the Pope, how many divisions could he deploy, it was the late Aneurin Bevan who hesitated to go naked into the conference chamber and the refusal in practice to treat all nations as equal is almost universally endorsed in the west; but for all that one of the most hopeful features of the world situation is the fact that more and more emergent nations assert their equality within the United Nations and cannot be prevented from doing so.

Addressing the annual conference of NATO parliamentarians in Paris on November 12, Vice-Admiral Smeeton of the Royal Navy, deputy supreme commander atlantic — and may I say in parenthesis that such a title in itself is a denial of the equal rights of nations – used these words: 'Besides having built a modern navy, the Russians have the largest fishing fleet in the world, and they are venturing on the high seas on a scale previously unknown in Russian history. There is only one conclusion: if we do not control the oceans the Communists will.'

There is no concept here of sharing which is the correlative of equality; there is simply 'Britannia rules the waves' handed over to NATO. Nor is this the voice of an irresponsible individual harking back to a forgotten past, it is an official voice pointing to the future and from no government or prime minister does there come one word of rebuke because, in the official mind, if the equalitarian language of the charter ever had any reality it has none now.

It is important to see together two simple facts: according to United Nations figures one in three of the world's population do not get enough to eat and, according to UNESCO figures, 700 million adults, two fifths of the world's adult population, are illiterate, and the figures are rising by 20 to 25 million every year. Here is to be seen the total absence of equality in the modern world and no serious move is being made to change the situation by what are called the major powers. The situation is challenged by the hungry and illiterate peoples themselves fighting for equality and establishing it, one by one, not with the help and assistance and encouragement of the dominant nations but against them. Those who have eyes to see must soon realise that the pink-faced people who call themselves white, who inhabit the western seaboards, are a minority of the world's population. They cannot expect to be treated as equals by the black, brown and yellow people who vastly outnumber them and who are now, with a cataclysmic rapidity and firmness, bursting both the material and spiritual shackles that have bound them, if they will not rapidly concede the equality that is demanded. The squalid treatment of the underdog which expects a courteous magnanimity when the roles are reversed reflects the plain stupidity not of an equal, but of an inferior mind. The times challenge to greatness while we clamour for easy chairs and cadillacs.

It is important to state as an addendum to this that chattel slavery, the most extreme form of inequality, still exists in the world. To give but one example, it is generally estimated that 10 per cent of the population of Arabia are slaves and it is in such countries as Aden, held under British 'protection', that this evil institution is most tenacious of life. The form of slavery known as debt-bondage is rife, serfdom and peonage continue: the sale of women into marriage is widespread. The spiritual destruction which slave owning wreaks upon the slave owner was demonstrated in the debate which took place in Bermuda in the 17th century as to whether slaves had souls. Baptism was sternly discouraged by the planters on the grounds that 'the breeding up of children in the Christian religion makes them stubborn.'[5] Nothing will remove slavery from human society but a general rising of the mass of the people of the countries concerned.

I have already said that when Tawney wrote his book it was the English scene with which he was concerned and his position about English society never changed. He put it in his last volume of essays:[6] 'In the interminable case of Dubb v Superior Persons & Co, whether Christians, capitalists or communists, I am an unrepentant Dubbite' and he went on to talk about the *Magnificat* and pulling the mighty down from their seats. The part which this country ought to play in world affairs on the side of equality can only be played by a virile society: for reasons which Tawney gave and which I have already mentioned the kind of society in which everybody pulls their full weight is one in which everybody is free to breathe an air which will expand their chests to the maximum and the only air which will do this is the air of equality. It follows that there is no task which is more urgent than of inquiring what is the position of this country in this matter today and then drawing any lessons which need to be drawn.

There is no doubt that conditions in Britain have improved during and since the second world war. The massive unemployment of the '30s has not yet recurred; the situation in which the majority of people who applied to join the army were rejected as physically unfit as the result of malnutrition no longer obtains: children no longer go to school without shoes. It is not, however, true that nobody is hungry and easy generalisations about 'the affluent society' obscure all too many awkward facts to which as little publicity as possible is given. The general level of advance, however, is not our concern: we are discussing equality and are therefore concerned with how far the level of advance is a level for all or how far there are significant pockets which are uncared for in the mass rush to secure any improvement that is possible in the general standard of living.

That there are such pockets is undeniable. The recent book by Peter Townsend, *The Last Refuge*, which is the result of a four-year investigation by a group of people, demonstrates conclusively that the treatment of the aged in public homes is a scandal of the first order. The number of people on national assistance is now almost 2,000,000. This figure is in itself staggering but it needs to be realised that in 76.5 per cent of cases those drawing relief from the board are supplementing other state benefits, either retirement pensions, sickness or industrial injury benefits, old-age pensions, widows' pensions and unemployment benefits. This in turn reveals the startling degree to which the so-called welfare state has already been whittled away, it being publicly admitted by the state that the old-age pensions and other benefits it pays are not enough to live on. It was stated indeed, in a declaration of the Bow Group, that benefits under state schemes should be reduced or at least not raised and then those so driven into an extreme of poverty dealt with by national assistance. While it is of course assumed that those in higher income groups should receive large pensions on retirement, it is not accepted that unskilled persons, who work at trades which do not have contributory pensions schemes, should receive from the community on their retirement a pension which is in any way adequate. Any kind of concept of equality is decisively rejected. Housing is a continuing sphere of inequality: the well-to-do can always buy a house, the poor find it increasingly difficult to rent the meanest flat. The number of those who are actually homeless goes up rather than down and in country villages for many miles around London the local agricultural workers are driven into council estates on the outskirts of the villages while the picturesque cottages they formerly inhabited are given over at high rents to the invading London middle class.

A Report on the Effects of the Rent Act in Greater London issued by the All-London Private Tenants Co-ordination Committee in 1961 stated: '. . . The Rent Act of 1957 was a bad act because it gave to all landlords the legal right to be bad landlords; because it gave encouragement to get-rich-quick speculators and takeover investment companies to force up land values and to exploit a basic necessity as though it were of no more importance than a detergent or a television set. And the minister camouflaged all this by proceeding on the widely publicised assumption (as unfounded now as when it was made in 1957) the market rent would, within a reasonable period, become fair rent, by virtue of increased building and the dispersal of tenants over a wider area. This has not happenend nor − during the life of the second series of three-year agreements − is it likely to happen.'

The gross inequity of the Rent Act, and the ruthless search for profit which motivated it, is perhaps equalled only by the readiness to risk the child welfare service of the London County Council, which no small local authority could emulate, and indeed its entire education service, for a politically motivated abolition of the LCC itself. It is when you take the measure of actions of this sort that you understand Tawney's approving quotation of the dictum of Maynard Keynes: 'Modern capitalism is absolutely irreligious.' [7]

We are concerned, however, not merely with certain pockets of poverty but with a mounting and general inequality. A Ministry of Labour survey made in 1961 showed that whereas in October 1960 630 manual workers in certain industries had in one week earned £50 or more, 18,804 had earned less than £7, whereas in between these two figures the majority ranged between £8 and £49. Big as these differences are, they are, of course, as nothing to the difference of income between any manual worker and those who use money as the one tool of their trade.

It was the president of the Royal Institute of British Architects, Sir Basil Spence, who, addressing the British architects' conference in Manchester in 1960 said: 'Like the profiteers who corner the bread supply in a besieged city, the speculators are cornering the limited supply of building land in town and country and holding the community up to ransom. The money that should be going into better architecture and higher standards is being taken by people who have contributed nothing to the building process. This has grown to the dimensions of a public scandal and threatens to make good planning and city reconstruction prohibitively expensive.'

This is but one symptom among many of the working of mammon in complete control. 'We feel bound to say in conclusion,' said the Royal Commission on Taxation in 1955, 'that the provision of untaxable benefits in kind is capable of becoming an abuse of the tax system.' Professor Titmuss in his *Income Distribution and Social Change* [8] provides overwhelming evidence that it has become such. Of 67 companies investigated by the British Institute of Management in 1960, 57 helped certain of their employees with house purchases; it was alleged by Viscount Monsell in the House of Lords in 1960 that flats were being let on expense accounts at £6,000 a year; nearly 50 per cent of all new motor cars are bought by business firms for their employees; at the top of the scale chauffeurs are provided as well as petrol; in 1955 the government estimated that 10 per cent (£33 million a year) of consumers' expenditure on wine and spirits was by business firms; much evidence is produced to show that only the taxfree expense account keeps the night club industry, and in particular the strip tease clubs, alive at all. The drug firms take a huge toll of the public health service: the economic power of insurance companies grows every year.

Professor Titmuss again put this in his *The Irresponsible Society*:[9] 'The last decade has witnessed something of an explosion in the accumulation of immense funds in the hands of private insurance companies and pensions trusts. The rate of growth in this control over the "economic surplus" may be even more dramatic in the next 10 years. Though there are many excuses, it is the relatively sudden impact and union of two major forces in western society which has led to this explosion, demographic change and economic growth. No-one who attempts to foresee the future of the public social services (to say nothing of economic freedom) in Britain, the USA, and other countries can now ignore this development.

'Although only meagre information has been published it would seem, in comparing New York and London stock exchange lists, that the percentage holding of equities by British insurance companies and pension funds was in 1957 already more than double the percentage holding of common stock by their opposite numbers of the USA. In other words, these institutions are twice as powerful in Britain as in America in terms of the ownership of industrial assets.'

Professor Titmuss's conclusion[10] is 'that we should be much more hesitant in suggesting that any equalising forces at work in Britain since 1938 can be promoted to the status of a "natural law" and projected into the future. As we have shown, there are other forces, deeply rooted in the social structure and fed by many complex institutional factors inherent in large-scale economies, operating in reverse directions. Some of the more critical of these factors, closely linked with the distribution of power, and containing within themselves the seeds of long-lasting effects – as, for instance, in cases of settlements and trusts – function as concealed multipliers of inequality. They are not measured at present by the statistics of income and only marginally by the statistics of wealth. Even so, there is more than a hint from a number of studies that income inequality has been increasing since 1949 whilst the ownership of wealth, which is far more highly concentrated in the United Kingdom than in the United States, has probably become still more unequal and, in terms of family ownership, possibly strikingly more unequal, in recent years.'

It needs only to be added that the desire to make it more unequal is rampant even among the supposedly responsible. An interesting example of this is to be found in the report published this month of the medical services review committee which regards as urgent 'the introduction of a medium-priced private bed in hopsitals' and the provision of drugs under the National Health Service for private patients as well as 'the acceptance of provident and insurance schemes in the assessment of tax.' In other words, provided I have enough money, I am to have a privileged position if I am ill. This is partly to be financed at the public expense and the money I spend on it myself, provided I am ready to lay it aside now rather than when I am actually taken ill, is to be exempt from income tax so that the real income gap between myself and the less fortunate is to be widened and I am to be the beneficiary in this. As a study in social responsibility it is to be recorded that the members of the committee making this report were appointed by the Royal Colleges of Physicians of London and Edinburgh, the Royal Colleges of Surgeons of England and Edinburgh, the Royal Faculty of Physicians and Surgeons of Glasgow, the Royal College of Obstetricians and Gynæcologists, the College of General Practitioners, the British Medical Association, and the Society of Medical Officers of Health.

These are certain tendencies, and the catalogue could be continued for a long time, in the economic background of 20th century Britain. Despite whatever advance we have made in social services, and it is an advance that has been more considerably checked in the last decade than many have realised and all the signs are that it will continue to be checked, we retain one of the most acutely class-divided societies in the world. We have a class system of education, we speak in class accents, we indulge class sport, we have a class stratification on railway trains, a class stratification in public houses, and even a class stratification in the graves in which our clay is deposited when we have shuffled off this mortal coil. In a survey called *House of Commons, 1959* published by *The Times* newspaper, it was show that, in that year, of the members of the House of Commons, 239 had been to Oxford and Cambridge as against only 96 who had been to other universities; that 222 had been to public schools and service colleges (and of these 164 to Eton or Harrow), whereas 138 had been to grammar and secondary schools and only 59 to elementary schools. Whereas the assembly in question contained 101 lawyers of one kind or another and 34 landowners or farmers, apart from 40 trade union officials there were only 32 who might possibly have been manual workers. The House of Commons, it seems, reflects reasonably accurately the general possibilities of rising to certain positions on the basis of having been to particular schools or having the kind of parentage or connections that might take you to certain professions. The overwhelming objection to all that this typifies is that it prevents the growth of real community; there can be no real fellowship between the members of the Athenæum and the habitués of the *Volunteer* off the Commercial Road and, if truth be told, in their heart of hearts, if not more overtly, the former despise the latter and the latter know it and react accordingly. There is bound to be restriction of production and a growing selfishness on the one side and nihilism on the other in an acutely class-divided society. Nor is it surprising that such a society begins to develop the diseased attitudes to racial minorities that are increasingly prevalent among us. Disease produces weakness and weakness is the breeding ground of disease.

If there are within our society deep-seated economic forces which work against equality and therefore in the deepest sense against the human future, where do other organised forces stand and what forces are there to battle for equality?

It is idle to look to the Conservative Party for a champion of equality. A party conceived in inherited wealth and nurtured on the pursuit of private gain, while it may have much to say about freedom, cannot reasonably be expected to forsake its entire ancestry. Its position is, indeed, quite explicit. In *Britain Strong and Free*[11] it said 'Socialists sneered and still sneer at what they call "imperialism," and think it no discredit that in their term of office countries have left the empire for the first time since the 18th century' — an explicit rejection of the United Nations' concept of the equality of peoples.

It went on to say: 'We must safeguard our traditional *way of life*. Conservatives believe in a society in which men and women from every section of the community and in every calling have a real chance of personal achievement. We do not believe in an egalitarian society centrally planned. . . . A worthwhile society cannot be established by Acts of Parliament and government planning. Adequate rewards for skill and enterprise and for the creation of wealth, belief that saving and investment are worthwhile, diffusion of property, home ownership, the rule of law, the independence of the professions, the strength of the family, personal responsibility and the rights of the individual — these are the true foundations of a free society.'

The words are honeyed but behind them stands the unequal society and the decay it breeds; behind them is the dictum of Professor Jones's *The Economics of Private Enterprise* of 1952:[12] 'The individual is assumed to be actuated by the motive of private gain which, in turn, can only be secured by supplying a public need. Private gain is the individual goal, public service the collective result.' It is an argument a Sunday School child could refute.

Professor Jones was a liberal and he expressed the basic reason why liberalism cannot save the society in which we live, and that is its inability to face the need of social ownership. The point was well expressed by Stephen Spender in 1937:[13] 'It is true that liberal democracy, which after nearly a century of haggling, gave the vote to the whole population, still has not freed the worker from economic bondage. All men are equal before the law; as Anatole France pointed out, the law impartially forbids the stealing of bread by rich and poor; it allows both rich and poor to sleep under bridges. Such freedom is a mockery perhaps, yet the Marxist or the Jew standing before the German Peoples' Court, whose birth or whose belief already condemns him, would be grateful for such a mockery. . . . The whole state advanced to the tune of liberal parliamentarianism for a hundred years; at the end of that time, although the lot of civilisation had materially improved, the gulf between rich and poor was greater than it had ever been. So political liberalism had failed, its failure being sealed with the Treaty of Versailles.'

There could be no more precise epitaph.

What then of Labour? 'The dominant issue of the 20th century is socialism,'[14] wrote Clement Attlee in 1937 and he finished his book with these words: 'A Labour government, not in a spirit of malice or revenge, but with the greatest regard for justice for all, must resolutely set about its task of rebuilding the life of this country on the principles of liberty, equality, and social justice, and of joining with other nations to create a world commonwealth.' The words are splendid and if you will browse through every Labour programme which has been issued since the war you will find words which are equally splendid. It would be tedious to quote; but for all that, despite its years of government and its period of opposition, Labour cannot be said either to have achieved an equal society or to be visibly leading towards one. If you attend a Labour Party conference you are in some sense in the world of the status-seekers and you can judge the importance within the hierarchy of labour of the person you are addresing by the hotel in which he stays. There is a Labour and trade union hierarchy, which of course is always provided with first class travel and first class hotel accommodation, and expects as by divine right to win all votes and insisits upon a voting system which is as inequitable as it is unreal but generally serves its purpose: and for all the sound declarations it is impossible to resist the conclusion that in practical terms the day-to-day world of labour is the world of inequality in its own particular form, and everybody knows it, and so there is no crusade and while this outlook continues there will be no crusade.

It is the absence of a flaming crusade for equality which has, in the past, led so many to the communist parties of the world, and the slogan 'Workers of the world, unite, you have nothing to lose but your chains' was certainly an equalitarian slogan. But equality, unhappily, fell into disrepute. Stalin's speech to the conference of leaders of industry of June 23, 1931,[15] is an important one in this regard. In it he pours scorn on 'Left equalitarinism in the sphere of wages' and states as one of his conclusions the necessity 'to abolish equalitarianism'. The fact has to be faced, and more than one Labour Party document in this country faces it, that this is not an easy matter to resolve. We need a society in which rewards are not measured by either the quantity or quality of the work done; we need to face the fact that there is something sordid and sub-human about a mathematical counting of what you give: equally we have to face the fact, as the Russians certainly did, that if you gave the same wage to a coal miner producing record quantities of coal as you did to a railway ticket collector you would not stimulate coal production. And that is all very well, up to a point, but once you take it too far and produce a striking difference in the way coalminers can rear their children and the way ticket collectors can rear their children you have struck a very serious blow at the kind of society you set out to produce. The Russians did this, and with that singleness of purpose which was one of the outstanding characteristics of Stalinism, the results of which some of us should have noted sooner than we did, the whole concept of equality was cast aside as a 'left deviation' and a whole caste of VIPs was produced and equality went overboard even in the relationships between one socialist country and another.

A document on *Basic Principles of International Socialist Division of Labour* adopted in June of this year by a meeting of representatives of the comunist and workers' parties of the member countries of the Council of Mutual Economic Assistance, held in Moscow, begins with these words: 'The world socialist system is a socialist economic and political community of free, sovereign nations. . . .' When it is, I venture to think that no power on earth will be able to stop its triumphant advancement in a way which will draw nation after nation into its orbit. But how true it is today the arrest of an Englishman in Hungary by Russians abundantly demonstrates. Here is not sovereignty or equality or freedom and it is the great tragedy of our epoch that party after party, movement after movement, country after country, dedicated to liberty, equality, fraternity, has either hauled down its flag, or else nailed it to the mast as a fraudulent symbol with which to ensnare the unwary.

Is there then nowhere we may turn? What of the Church, the Church founded on 'Blessed are the poor, blessed are the meek, blessed are they that suffer for righteousness sake'? It is not for me to talk of the Free Churches, so-called, which have, no doubt, both their freedom and their bondage. But the Church which it is my duty to serve, the Church endowed and established, does not believe in equality: it believes, jointly with the Church of Rome, in a concept of hierarchy which is false, a notion which has no basis in primitive Christianity and which combines today with the fact of establishment to imprison and shackle the equalitarian creed the Church exists to proclaim. When, in 1940, Tawney wrote a preface to a reprint of Gore's Essex Hall Lectures, *Christianity Applied to the Life of Men and Nations*, he stressed the necessity of disestablishment for the spiritual health of the Church because, otherwise, it was tied 'to the whole legal and penal system, with all its preferences for the claims of property to those of personality.' He was right. In all the *furore* today about the need of reforming the *Book of Common Prayer* nobody ever mentions the need of removing that most disgraceful of all the prayers it contains in the Prayer for the Church Militant in the holy communion service: 'Grant unto her whole council, and to all that are put in authority under her, that they may truly and indifferently minister justice, to the punishment of wickedness and vice, and to the maintenance of thy true religion and virtue.' Has there ever been a state that needed the incitement of the Church to the imposition of savage sentences on the unfortunate? Does a state which has the Criminal Justice Act on its statute book need such incitement? Is not the role of the Church to plead for mercy? What kind of 'religion and virtue' can be maintained by law? Again in the rising and righteous clamour to do something about the 39 Articles I have yet to hear one person question Article 38: 'The riches and goods of Christians are not common, as touching the right, title, and possession of the same as certain Anabaptists do falsely boast.' The Anabaptists will yet come into their own.

It is forgotten that even when Christians first spoke of hierarchy the bishop, who was elected by his flock, was not only the shepherd of a far smaller flock than the Anglican bishop possesses today but he could not govern by himself. He could issue no diocesan canon without the assent of a synod of presbyters and sometimes, and rightly, of laity as well. And for all the 19th century talk of the monarchial episcopate no such thing ever existed in the history of the Church until after the Reformation and then, I suspect, only in the Church of England. You have only to add to this historical abuse the use of that mediæval atrocity of 'My Lord' for a Christian bishop and you have laid a snare which few souls may be expected to survive. 'Christ,' said St Clement,[16] 'is of those who are humble-minded, and not of those who exalt themselves over his flock.'

Our search for the apostles of equality fails today at whatever point of the compass we look: a firm determined band of people who see that equality is the very foundation of the City of God, the City which lieth four-square; who see that it is the promise of the future as it is also the sword by which we must march to the future as a band of comrades able to wield the sword with abandon in a fight against the world of inequality which is strangling the human spirit; such a band does not exist. It ought to exist in more places than one, but it does not. The need for it grows: equality between black and white, equality between national states, which is the only possible prelude to the transcendence of national states in world unity, the equality of human beings not simply 'before the law,' but in the street and the pub and the train, in the real world in which they live and in which they have to create community; these are the majestic needs of our time. It follows that they will be met.

A book was published last year on behalf of the Christian Frontier Council called *Equality and Excellence*. It was written by Daniel Jenkins and with considerable discernment it postulated the need of equality in the modern world but saw a problem in relating equality to excellence. Tawney never saw this problem. To him excellence flowed naturally out of equality; people who lived as comrades in fellowship would naturally flower and blossom. I have no doubt at all that Tawney was right and that the Christian Frontier Council need not worry, it needs only to fight. To say this is not to underestimate a very valuable book; but a concluding essay within it, by David Edwards, called 'Equality as part of our heritage' lends itself to much misunderstanding when it talks of 'the Bible and equality.' 'The idea of equality as rooted in modern political discussion is not to be found within it' we are told, although it is admitted that we find, with various degrees of clarity, some statement of the reality lying behind the idea. Mr Edwards would do well to read again the Mosaic Laws of the Pentateuch based on an equalitarian system of land ownership and a general equality of the Jew before the law: he might gain from a re-reading of the prophets with their vision of a world of complete equality in which even the lion would lie down with the lamb. As to the New Testament, the Beatitudes; the Sermon on the Mount; *The Acts of the Apostles* with the Church having all things common; the Epistles written to 'the saints' who are equals under Christ, for in Christ Jesus 'there is neither Greek nor Jew, male nor female, bond nor free'; the *Revelation* with the City of God of which equality is the keynote: have our modern theological colleges turned all this grandeur simply into a mass of syllables which pour from the tongue in one unrelated blasphemy after another?

At the beginning of this lecture I pointed out that the word equality was not to be confused with the word 'same': that it was a value judgment between persons. It can be described very simply indeed: if there are three human beings and one sits down to dinner and another waits upon him and another gets down on his knees and licks up the crumbs which fall from the rich man's table, they are not behaving as equals. When they sit down at the table and eat together, however different their talents or their experiences, even though they speak different languages, they are equal. But Christianity is the religion of the common table, or it is nothing. Its chief sacrament is the perpetual memorial of the last supper where food is taken and broken and wine is poured and blessed and then all come and participate on terms of utter and complete equality. So is the life of God given perpetually to a divided world. You cannot buy your way in: you cannot grasp more than your neighbour: there is no order of precedence: there is − equality, and this equality is a reality by which men and women live and a prophecy of how they shall live.

I say that this is what happens. There is, I fear, one exception. When members of the Royal Family attend the holy communion outside the royal chapels it appears to be the practice that they do not come to the communion rails with the rest of the congregation: communion is taken to them privately before the others in the place in which they already kneel: they take priority over the holy communion itself. If this unhappy practice does not ovethrow the nature of the sacrament it certainly frustrates the purpose of the sacrament which is to establish a communion between God and people and people themselves, which this act denies. It cannot be regarded as conducive to the spiritual health of any concerned in it: it remains true that as our humanity is common so is our mortality and

> 'sceptre and crown must tumble down,
> and in the dust be equal made
> with the poor crooked scythe and spade.'

Equality is the clear, essential teaching of the New Testament. It was carried on by the fathers. Even Lactantius had no doubt about it. Look at the 15th and 16th chapters of the 5th Book of the *Divine Institutes*. The first part of justice, he says, is *pietas*. The second part is *æquitas* − the temper which teaches people to put themselves on an equality with others. Cicero, he reminds us, called it *æquabilitas*. God, who inspires men and women, wished them all to be equal. He made them all for virtue and promised them all immortality. No one, in the sight of God, can be a slave or a master; He is the Father of all and all are His children. So he criticises Roman and Greek institutions for not recognising the principle of equality. Ambrosiaster in his *Commentary on the Colossians* has a long passage in which he attributes slavery to sin and insists that God makes all people free and equal. Augustine[17] insists that God did not make rational man to lord it over his rational fellows but only to be master of the irrational creatures, and that in the order of divine creation people are free and equal and the slaves neither of man nor of sin. At a much later date Gregory the Great[18] reminds masters that their slaves are their equals through their share in one human nature.

This insistence could not be otherwise beacause Christianity takes the matter much farther than this. It insists that equality is the nature of God Himself. 'In this Trinity none is afore or after other: none is greater, or less than another, but the whole three persons are coeternal together, and coequal.'[19] It was exactly this that was denied by Arius. To him Jesus was, essentially, the first of the creatures. He was, therefore, not like the Father in essence nor the Father's true Word or Wisdom. He does not perfectly or accurately know either the Father or his essence, and like all the creatures, he is by nature capable of change. 'The essences of the Father and the Son and the Holy Spirit,' he said, 'are separate in nature, and estranged, and disconnected, and alien, and without participation in each other . . . utterly unlike each other in essence and glory, into infinity.' God was first 'alone and solitary'. The Son is a being altogether by himself 'and has no fellowship with the nature of the Father.' 'He is not equal, no, not one in essence with Him.' 'Foreign from the Son is the essence of the Father.' One of the things which Athanasius denounced in his *Orations* as impiety, was the idea that the Son 'has no fellowship with the nature of the Father,' for this would mean no fellowship between people and God, between people and perfection, with the corollary that humanity must remain forever debased and subordinate. The Father, said Athanasius, 'is the Light, the King, the Universal Governor.' The son, himself Man, must be these things too. The Son, he said, 'did not receive the titles of Son and of God as the reward of his good offices on our behalf; but he condescended to humble himself so low that he might raise us to the position of his brethren. He vouchsafed to be made man in order to make men like God.' And here is the heart of the Christian concept of equality − that people are called through Christ to God who through equality and fellowship is ultimate and eternal perfection.

All who can see the merest shadow of this glory have but one vocation − to live in the crusade for equality which in this last hour must become the torch which lights us to truth, and freedom, and peace, which lights us to humanity because it is the path to God.

Equality is of God and is eternal. It is our nature and it is indestructible. It is life, and after winter it must burst through the veins of men and women, and then stand up they must and march into their future.

What is this, the sound and rumour? What is this that all men hear,
Like the wind in hollow valleys when the storm is drawing near,
Like the rolling on of ocean in the eventide of fear?
  'Tis the people marching on.

This lecture was given in November, 1962.

References

1 *Equality* 1931 edition p 23.
2 ibid chapter 2.
3 ibid chapter 3.
4 ibid chapter 7.
5 H. C. Wilkinson, *The Adventurers of Bermuda*. Oxford. 1958. pp 359–360.
6 *The Attack & Other Papers*. 1953. p 164.
7 *Religion and the Rise of Capitalism*. 1926 edition, p 286.
8 London, 1962.
9 Fabian Society, 1960. p 13.
10 *Income Distribution and Social Change*. p 198.
11 Conservative and Unionist Central Office. 1951.
12 p 144.
13 *Forward from Liberalism*. pp 38–39.
14 *The Labour Party in Perspective*. London, 1937. p 15. p 287.
15 Stalin. *Leninism*. Vol 2. 1933. London. pp 428–31.
16 *First Epistle*. Chapter 16.
17 *City of God*. 19. 15.
18 *Liber Pastoralis Curæ*. 3. 5.
19 *Athanasian Creed*.

Charles Coulson
Responsibility

I must begin with a confession. I did not have the privilege of knowing Tawney personally; I heard him speak, I believe, only once. But like many others in my generation I was very considerably influenced by what he wrote. It would come to me as no surprise to be told that there are some echoes, reflections of things that were his, in what I want to say about responsibility. The first Tawney lecture was centred round equality, and in it Stanley Evans spoke of the only adequate basis for the practice of equality as being rooted in our common status as children of God. But this is only the starting point. How do we express this equality in the lives of people and of communities? Whence comes the dynamic that converts a principle into a movement? Inevitably equality passes into responsibility.

This is not to suggest that people have never thought about responsibility. A few months ago I attended a meeting of the central committee of the World Council of Churches in Nigeria. One of the things which we were commissioned to do was to make plans for a world conference on the relation between the Christian faith and modern society. One of our members had the temerity to suggest that if we were to deal with this conjunction of faith and society, the word 'responsibility' should appear in the title. He was howled down, with the *déjà-vu* assumption: 'We have used that word so much lately that we dare not put it into the title of an international world conference.' If this comment were valid, and Christian communities were to stop thinking and talking about responsibility, it would be a sad day. For there is no other aspect of life which shows people to be so much human as the way they exercise responsibility.

Think of it in this way. Thanks to the scientific development of electrical circuits and the like, it is now possible to devise machines with quite wonderful powers. There is no difficulty, in principle, in designing a machine that will invent new things, that will learn by its own mistakes, that will even be able to reproduce itself. But no one has suggested that we can design a machine that will consciously exercise responsibility. This is why any significant thinking about responsibility is ultimately thinking about what makes us really and truly human; and its right excercise the best indication of our humanity.

The qualifying phrase — 'right' exercise — is important; its elaboration is the chief subject matter of this lecture. For when I think about the nature of the world in which we all of us live, or the times in which we live in it, I grow very much aware that the area in which our responsibility must be exercised is now greatly widened. It is of this widening that I must speak. And with the widening comes a note of urgency. If those of us who are Christian, or, though perhaps not professing official Christianity have come to see the claims that true humanism makes[1], do not explore this new area in which Christian responsibility should be exercised, then it is unlikely that the rest of the world will do so. And the opportunities for the full human life, which we believe it is God's intention that every one should enjoy, will be diminshed.

Let me, therefore, deal first with the collective responsibility that accompanies those recent developments, particularly technological and scientific, which are the characteristic of our generation. It will not be hard to show that society is now called to a new and imaginative way of looking at some of our present world problems. Then let me turn to the scientists, through whose effort the possibility of constructive action is now possible. We must consider to what extent they are involved in decision-making and how they themselves look at their responsibility. This will naturally lead us to the final part of this study, which is the way in which all of us are involved in setting the pattern of thought within which not only the scientific community but also our society as a whole, including government, has to exercise its proper judgment.

The responsible society

The descriptive phrase 'the responsible society' is, I believe, largely the product of specialist committees within the World Council of Churches. At the very first general assembly of the world council, at Amsterdam in 1948, soon after the end of world war II, the report of section III has these words: 'A responsible society is one where freedom is the freedom of people who acknowledge responsibility to justice and public order, and where those who hold political authority or economic power are responsible for its exercise to God and the people whose welfare is affected by it.'

This is all right as a beginning. It certainly sets responsible behaviour within a context of religious belief and so frees it from the claims of temporal history or the fashion of political ideology. But it does not go far enough. It does not ask sufficiently fundamental questions about the nature of political authority and economic power; and it does not recognise the very intimate dependence of all parts of the world upon one another. For the most important thing to be said about the world as a whole, in this century, is that it is one world.

'Whether it is recognised or not,' writes A. T. Eastman[2], 'whether it is welcomed or not, world citizenship has been automatically conferred upon every single resident of this shrinking globe by the irreversible events of our age. To qualify that universal citizenship with the adjective *Christian*, means basically to add the element of perspective, responsibility and zest. For the alert and committed Christian of this new world is one who sees the hand of God in the coming great civilisation, who knows that he or she is called by God both to discover and to shape the society to come, and who believes that this is the most exciting of all times in which to live and work under the providence of God.'

Christians have no right to be surprised that it is one world now in which we live. In a sense they have known it, spiritually, right from the beginning. But now to its spiritual unity has been added material and, soon, cultural unity also: modern technology sees to that. If I go from London to New York, my modern jet plane takes two and a half hours, as judged by local times in the two cities. This means, for example, that news reels, taken one morning in London, can be shown all over

America that afternoon. Almost the whole world was present at the funeral service of Winston Churchill. When the new Concord jet liner is built and it fulfils its promise to travel at 2,000 miles an hour, the flying time from London to New York will be one and a half hours. We shall arrive in New York three and a half hours earlier than we leave London — judged, of course, by local time.

This is just one example — and perhaps not a very novel one — to illustrate our need to think now in global terms. The whole world has becomne one backyard, so that any attempt by any nation to express its responsibility in national terms is to deny this fundamental new fact of our modern life. There is an immediate corollary of this, which is the cause of a good deal of the distress of thought in the councils of nations. In the old days, when news travelled slowly, it was perfectly possible for relative wealth, and relative poverty, to exist side by side. We do well to remember that it is only 100 years since an American congressman, who arrived not more than a month after the opening of congress, was counted early! This situation is completely changed. Every part of the world knows what is happening in every other part. 'A kiss in Cadiz is heard in Canton.' So it is no longer possible for disparities to exist without the sufferers knowing of their condition. I shall have to say quite a lot about this, partly from my own personal experience and partly because I believe it to be central to many of the major world problems of today.

In this widening of responsibility judgments and decisions have to be taken, not by one person but by a community. To some extent this may begin in the individual response of one person: 'The church can be most effective in society as it inspires its members to ask in a new way what their Christian responsibility is whenever they vote or discharge the duties of public office, whenever they influence public opinion, whenever they make decisions as employers or as workers or in any other vocation to which they may be called.'[3] We are familiar with this personal involvement in politics and society through the work of some of the early Christian socialists, people like F. D. Maurice, Charles Kingsley, J. M. Ludlow, Scott Holland and Scott Lidgett. We may not always follow the light that we see, but at least those lamps have been lit. Now, however, we must add to the old personal involvement a new community one.

I will illustrate this by choosing an example that is fresh in my mind, since I saw it last month in west Africa. Nigeria is a new country — in the sense that only relatively recently has it acquired its independence. It is attempting, in common with all the newly-born countries of Africa, to telescope into one or two decades the progress which has taken the older countries of the west 200 years. As a consequence of this rapid social and technical change one finds most curious contrasts. A few vignettes will soon show what I mean.

A doctor friend in a remote region is keeping some medical statistics. They are possibly the only reliable medical statistics in that great country; and they show that 50 per cent of the children born in Nigeria die before the age of five. Those of us who have children of our own can soon judge what that means in terms of human distress. My wife and I have four children, all well and healthy. If we had been Nigerian, only two of them would have lived to their fifth birthday. Even this is a better record than in some places. In Brazil, for example, the fifth largest country in the world, and instrinsically of fabulous wealth, poverty kills 2,000 people every day. 'In one year more children die in Brazil than the total number of children killed by bombs and Nazi ghettos in world war II. In one neighbourhood of a Brazilian city, 500 out of 1,000 children born die during their first day of life. In another city, in one of the poorest sections of the country, no child born in the last four years has survived. . . . These people do not die — they are strangled by the shameful conditions of poor housing, malnutrition and complete lack of social or economic assistance.[4] '

To return to Nigeria — in order that living conditions should be improved, its government recognises the need for higher education. Another university was started, but had to be stopped because there was no money in the public coffers. There must also be an airforce. But aeroplanes are terribly costly, and building an airport is even more expensive than buying aeroplanes. Social services are desirable. But there are no doctors. My own doctor friend told me that his nearest professional colleague was 30 miles away, so that he was responsible medically for about 1,000 square miles. (This is not unique to Africa. It is just the same in the villages of India.)

This little picture of Nigeria shows a country trying to establish itself. But it finds that it cannot do so. It comes to realise — as of course we know theoretically very well — that the disparity betweeen the richer and the poorer countries is actually increasing. Even the help that has been given has depreciated: for example, since 1950, 26 billion dollars of aid has been given to the underdeveloped countries (among which is Nigeria). We may use the words 'give to': but in fact more than half of the gift has entirely disappeared without achieving anything. This is because the price has dropped that is paid by the rich developed countries for the primary products upon whose sale the underdeveloped countries have to depend. And, at the same time, the price which they have had to pay for the machinery and other equipment which they are obliged to import from the highly-developed countries, has risen. This gap alone threatens to reach an annual 20 billion dollars by the end of the present decade.[5]

It seems to me that a truly responsible society today would be one that recognised this situation and, having recognised it, did something significant about it. For, if we are all members of one family, they are my brothers and sisters who live in Nigeria; they are my brothers and sisters who sleep with two million others on the pavements of Calcutta; they are my children who die in Brazil — every one of them. When we begin like this, we think not only of the unemployed on Tyneside, or the orphans in our National Children's Homes, but also that we belong to all these others too. But there is a difference. We can discharge our responsibility to the deprived few of our own country in an almost personal and private way, and — anyhow — the welfare state has made many earlier types of charity redundant. We can discharge our responsibility to the deprived multitudes elsewhere, of whose predicament we can no longer plead ignorance, only by sustained, corporate thought and decision.

It will be clear that I am not thinking of any emotional manoeuvre when I urge the necessity of solid thinking. Without this, community decisions may well prove inadequate and sterile. Yet the magnitude of western society's responsibility here is staggering. Let us think for a moment of some of the capital needs of the underdeveloped countries. This will soon reveal the contrast with ourselves. Thus, there is one particular committee of the London County Council with an annual budget of 23 million pounds. We may compare this with the eastern region of Nigeria where the annual budget – for everything – is only 25 million pounds. This shows the scale in which we have to think. The future of these parts of the world must depend on a considerable development of industry. To establish one person in heavy industry requires between five and 10 thousand pounds. In light industry the figure is less, between two and five thousand pounds. We have only to multiply these figures by the numbers of people who must ultimately be established in industrial jobs and factories, to realise that even in a country the size of Nigeria, something like 25 thousand million pounds must be made available. Since this figure represents about five hundred pounds for every person in Britain, and since the population of Nigeria is only a fraction of that of India, it is clear that this is a collective responsibility, of far too great a magnitude to be achieved by individual effort.

This makes me ask if there is any significant sign that our own country is taking the matter seriously. We do not need to be party political here, for neither of the major political parties in Britain can boast of what they have done. Seven years ago at the general election, the socialist party publicly proposed that one per cent of our national income should be used for this purpose. However, this is nothing like enough, and was not a really responsible decision. The precise percentage that could be efficiently given and properly used is very hard to estimate. In principle we can help best with a vigorous national economy in Britain. This must provide commodities for the home market if it is to be able to produce the necessary capital equipment for abroad; and there is a rather stringent limit to the rate at which an underdeveloped economy is able to absorb new capital. It may well be that something like three or four per cent of our national income is the maximum that could profitably, and effectively, be used in this way. However, even this figure is a great deal larger than has been seriously proposed by any political party in this country.

It is no good saying that we shall do this later – or when our productivity has increased – or when we can lower the income tax. The urgency of which I spoke earlier requires that we start doing it now. Here is a report[6] from Joan Chapman who, in Basutoland, had just met the local Save the Children Fund treasurer, recently returned from India. 'The first thing he said was how lucky the people of Basutoland were – compared with India. But even so it is pointless telling hungry people that there are people worse off than they are. His most touching story was about a man dying of starvation who was too weak to eat the food a nun brought him, and his last words were, "You should have come yesterday".' This is a poignant reminder that the need has got to be met by an immediate response. Many of the less developed parts of the world are going down on an absolute scale; on a relative scale this is true for all of them.

This is not the place to elaborate a more detailed practical policy to be the expression of our concern. But one or two things must be said, if only to show the need for national-level planning. I referred earlier to the way in which countries like our own contrive to pay less and less for the primary products from underdeveloped countries, at the same time that they have to pay more for the machinery and tools which they are obliged to import from us. In one sense, therefore, we are doubly unjust. But 'we' means not only Britain; all the developed and industrial countries are in this racket. I believe that in this situation responsibility should mean that we look for a fair price for the primary products that we import. If it is true that Ghana depends to a large extent on the sale of the cocoa that it can export, then we should not endanger its standard of living by refusing to buy except at cut-price levels.

There was a time, in the Middle Ages, when the church exercised this power, and decreed what was a 'just price'. It is no longer the task of the church to do this, nor indeed has the church, as such, the ability to make this kind of judgment. But I am quite certain that the church ought to make sure that someone does. If it were to result, as it almost certainly would, in our bars of chocolate costing us a little more, this would still be the right thing. Decisions as to what constitutes a just price are necessarily partly subjective: they must therefore be taken out of the hands of those who profit most by paying less than the just price. There seems no likely way in which this sort of control can be exercised without government supervision and government powers. We dare not leave this to private enterprise (though shortly I shall refer to other aspects in which private enterprise can help greatly). This need not surprise us, accustomed as we became during the last war to controls of all kinds. The sooner that the problems of which I speak are admitted to be on the same level of importance as war, the sooner are we likely to accept the necessary strategy.

Our British record in this field does not always compare favourably with that of other countries. An enquirer might be surprised to be told that if a comparison is made between the amount of money that we actually give and the amount that we lend (and hope to get back with interest), the ratio for Britain is smaller than for almost any other major country. I can only conclude that the acquisitive society is still with us, and I know that Tawney would want to say about it.

This does not mean that nothing is being done; for there is action, often in conjunction with local government in the receiving countries, and often also with the aid of private enterprise. It may seem distateful to many people that private enterprise, so often execrated as the fountainhead of old-style imperialism, should be useful in this way. But if the fact is that private enterprise has the vitality, and the know-how, and the access to suitable markets, then it would be deeply wrong to adopt any doctrinaire position, and refuse to participate nationally. One example of such cooperation is the Commonwealth Development Corporation, which specialises in the promotion of local development corporations for industry and agriculture, and local building societies for housing – three major needs in any developing country. When any project has proved successful, the CDC share is sold out to further local ownership and the money can then be used to start another enterprise somewhere else. Here there is no ideology to defend or national axe to grind[7]. It is of interest that large charities such as Oxfam have lately adopted a 'rolling' scheme of this kind for several of their projects, the return from one project being used as a repayable loan to start off another.

There are situations, however, where private enterprise companies, while inevitably looking for a profit, can nevertheless help in the development of independent schemes. In Nigeria, recently, I learnt that the Israelis have put up 49 per cent of the capital for a television and wireless service. This leaves the majority control in the hands of the Nigerians, as of course we all know that it should be. In other parts of Africa both American and British industries are investing capital in development, with the proviso that a part of this capital is written off each year, so that in 20 years' time the whole of the business belongs to the underdeveloped country. This kind of action, unhappily still too infrequent, shows one way in which the promotion of local industry, and the development of indigenous business skills, may express corporate responsibility.

There are many difficulties in this. Most projects in this category are of enormous magnitude, needing action at government level. It is revealing that UNESCO will not now tackle any project in which less than half a million pounds (1.5 million dollars) are involved. Professor Blackett has put it in these terms[8]. 'In addition to likely commercial and government short-term lending, an additional £1,000 million a year is needed as a free gift, or as long-term loans, from the 400 million rich westerners to the 1,000 million Asians, Africans and South Americans in the underdeveloped countries outside the society orbit.'

Unfortunately governments are not very good at actions of this sort. Who can forget that at the general election seven years ago, one of the two major political parties used as its slogan, 'You've never had it so good,' and the other, unwilling to be outdone in this appeal to self-interest, responded, 'If you vote for us you'll have it better'. We stand condemned. Why was it that the Christian community of that time kept silent, when it should have been the first to say: 'A plague on both of you! This is no way to modern corporate responsibility.'

The responsibility of the scientist

It is quite obvious that many of the possibilities just outlined have become possibilites only because of the phenomenal discoveries of science. The scientist is often charged with opening a modern Pandora's box, releasing into an unwilling and ill-prepared world all the evils from which now people seek to escape. This is a gross misjudgment. It is my own experience that among all the different groups of people with whom I have been involved, the scientific group, *as a whole*, is the one most aware of this responsibility. It is a tragedy to have to confess that if I wanted to be among a group of people who would feel in their bones a responsibility for what was going on around them, I would not choose a church audience: I would choose a scientific one. This does not mean British scientitsts, alone; but scientists from all over the world. I think now of an international conference to which I went seven or eight years ago, in Yugoslavia, behind the iron curtain. Some 150 distinguished scientists were there from both sides of this curtain and they represented almost all shades of political thought. Yet almost the first unofficial thing that they did was to propose an open meeting to discuss scientific responsibility.

It has always been like that. Leonardo da Vinci invented a submarine but, because he felt that such knowledge would be used for evil purposes, he did not make it known. Robert Boyle, one of the most distinguished early members of the Royal Society (whose charter enjoined on the fellows that they should devote their scientific talents 'to the glory of God and the welfare of the human race'), invented some poisons and a form of invisible ink, which he refused to divulge. The Italian Tartaglia devised a new and better form of gunnery but declined to make it known to the armies and the generals because they would use such knowledge for evil purposes. Even in the matter of nuclear weapons, 'most of the physicists who have had contact with atomic weapons are deeply disturbed. Most of them are very sensitive to moral values. At the same time it is difficult for them to know what to do. There is enormous public pressure on scientists to do in the laboratories the utmost that science is capable of doing.'[9] And Michael Faraday asked by the British government about the possible use of poison gas against the French in the nineteenth century, replied that this was certainly possible but he would have nothing whatever to do with such a thing.

Scientists themselves do feel strongly about these issues. But, if they can bring no other insights to bear on the making of a decision, they will inevitabley be at a loss. People can only exercise responsibility when they believe themselves accountable to some authority above themselves. Science, in itself, does not provide that authority. So scientists are in as much need of guidance and support, when they come to decide that they will do with their discoveries, as is anyone else. It is not fair to blame the scientist for a situation where, in one sense, all of us — scientist and non-scientist — are guilty. It is only when the climate of thought in the society in which we live is sensitive to issues of this kind that any group within that society can function properly. No amount of scientific expertise can compensate for spiritual blindess and lethargy. [10]

We do well to remember that when a discovery is first made, it is highly unlikely that the discoverer will be able to foresee the fullness of its later application. Not often does the scientist foresee as uncannily as Lord Rutherford when, in Manchester at the end of world war I, he wrote to an American friend telling him about his research on the artificial disintegration of the nucleus of an atom. He added that he thought it possible that ultimately this discovery might turn out to be as significant as the war then drawing to its bitter close. Most of us would accept the view of the American physicist P. W. Bridgman, that if he had to guarantee that none of his discoveries were ever to be used wrongly, he would need to become a personal pressure-group in Washington, lobbying congress, and then alternating back to his laboratory. That sort of life is quite impossible and only in rare cases would it lead to great discoveries.

This is not to say that scientists never do express a collective responsible judgment. They often do. For example it is not as widely known as it should be[11] that among the group working at Chicago on the atomic bomb project, a secret poll was conducted to discover what the scientists themselves felt to be the right course of action with this dreadful weapon. A few days before the first experimental test in New Mexico, only 15 per cent voted to use atomic bombs, 'in the manner that is from the military point of view most effective in bringing about prompt Japanese surrender at minimum human cost to our armed forces.' The other 85 per cent may not have been able to agree on what should have been done. But that, as I said before, is as much our responsibility as theirs. In the event it was President Truman who decided to use the bomb — as his autobiography is at some pains to make clear.

When criticising scientists it is easy to use hindsight and wonder why, in view of what subsequently happened, a different decision was not taken. The difficulty for scientists is that they must use their judgment without knowing the future. Here they may be right or they may be wrong. We may say that, in the spirit that I have just been describing, they are under obligation to act responsibly, using their judgment as well as they can, in estimating the likely results of their work. Here there will not often be any clear-cut absolutes, defining codes of right and wrong. Circumstances themselves will change and what appears wrong today may have a new colour tomorrow or in 10 years.

I may perhaps be allowed a personal illustration of this apparent ambiguity. At the end of World War II it happened that, in the course of my own work on the behaviour of electrons, I knew more than anyone else about some of the properties of graphite. Now graphite is a substance which can be used in a nuclear pile to slow down the fast-moving neutrons and make them more effective in causing the nuclear fission process to continue. So, almost overnight, graphite became an exceedingly important substance. Before long, even though the information that I possessed was not in itself of very great significance scientifically, I was visited by groups from different countries, asking me if I would join up in research teams where this sort of thing was being studied in more detail.

It would have been nice to exchange the relative poverty of a university for the unlimited resources and equipment of a government defence research group. Scientists are human beings, who must live, and who find a quite proper satisfaction in the discoveries with which they are associated. Offers of this kind are seductive, particularly to a young man not yet firmly established on the scientific ladder. I had to think as clearly as I could, and ask myself for what purpose my aid was being sought. According to my judgment at that time, these purposes were such that I could not approve. I might be right, or I might be wrong but, since on the day that I became a Christian, I also became a Christian pacifist, I could not believe in any use of nuclear knowledge which facilitated the development of atomic bombs. It seemed to me then that this would be the prime motive in my invitation, so I could not do anything but decline. Furthermore, I felt it necessary to switch my research to another topic without this liability.

There is an interesting end to this episode. Ten years later, in Oxford, there was a young postdoctoral research student from America working with me. He came to me one day and asked me to suggest a problem on which he could work, under my direction. Without thinking, I outlined the problem of the vibrating patterns in a crystal of graphite. So he started and I began to help him. Then − suddenly − the thought crossed my mind: 'Good heavens, what are you doing! In 1945 you moved away from graphite and began to work in quite a different field and here you are, 10 years later, putting someone to work on it, in a closely related part of the subject!' But of course there was a difference between 1945 and 1955. For during that period all the knowledge that was needed for the making of nuclear bombs had been obtained and at least two countries were in the position of being able to over-kill. What, rightly or wrongly, I judged to be irresponsible for me in 1945, had become responsible in 1955. This does not mean that there are no rules of conduct, no blacks and whites in the making of a decision. It does mean that even if the principles on which we act have an unchanging character, they way in which those principles are expressed will change in the flux of historical situation.

If there were any moral to be drawn from this incident it must be that the scientist deserves more understanding and spiritual support in the making of decisions than we have sometimes been willing to give. This is particularly the case in relation to large-scale government science, where the appeals of novelty and priority and loyalty combine to make responsible decision difficult. Some recent experiments in space research are illuminating here.[12] In the first of these — Operation Starfish — the US government exploded a 1.4 megaton hydrogen bomb 250 miles above Johnson Island in the Pacific. Despite earlier protests from groups of impartial scientists, who maintained that the proposed test would substantially prejudice astrophysical and geophysical science and create an unnecessary hazard for manned space flights, the American government persisted. In the event it seems that we may now have 'to wait more than 30 years before the natural electron fluxes in the region around 1.5 earth radii can be measured with complete freedom from artificial effects.' Several satellites were subsequently damaged extensively by the new radiation belt thus created. The Christian will say of this, that it was at best an irresponsible misuse of the providence of God.

A second example is Project West Ford in which, as a means of establishing an invulnerable, world-wide, military communications system, the earth was to be encircled by thin belts of very fine copper wires. These would act as radio mirrors and be physically indestructable. Again, despite previous protests by independent scientists, the experiment was attempted in October, 1961. Fortunately — as we now know — the package of fine bits of wire failed to disperse as intended and the world of astronomical research was not hampered, as it would otherwise have been.

In both these examples a government has carried on with proposed large-scale experiments, despite protests and counter-arguments, on the grounds that the knowledge to be obtained from them was of military value. But of course it was also exciting and, as Professor J. R. Oppenheimer once said, 'If a project is technically sweet, there will usually be someone willing to partake in it'. Responsible action here is more difficult. All too easily we reach the situation described by Hans Bethe to a US congressional committee: 'We did not think until too late.'

Individual responsibility

I turn now to the third section of this lecture, in which we pass from the large-scale responsibility of government and the peculiar responsibility of the scientific community, to the responsibility of ordinary mortals. There is a wide range of answer to be given to the question: what can I do in the new environment of today? Not all of what I say will apply to everyone but, in one way or another, everything should apply to someone.

Let us begin with Africa, a great country in ferment. UNESCO recently carried out a survey of some of Africa's major needs. One of these is obviously education, and the present bottleneck in the provision of qualified personnel. UNESCO estimates that 'the African states will need between now and 1970, 200,000 additional secondary school teachers, ... in the field of higher education it is estimated that Africa will, between now and 1980, need 7,000 expatriate university teachers apart from those being trained in the 35 university institutions being developed in Africa.'[13]

When in Nigeria I had a personal opportunity of seeing what is at present being done by organisations such as Voluntary Service Overseas, International Voluntary Service (which is the earliest of all this group) and the American Kennedy Peace

Corps. In parts of the northern region these volunteers have literally kept secondary education from complete collapse. I felt proud to see this. But when I remembered those earlier figures of need, I began to wonder whether there were not a call for many more individuals. I knew the need. Even young men and women who have just left school and are waiting to go to a British university a year later would be welcomed with open hands. It seemed to me that here was an opportunity for the Christian church which should be gladly accepted. Perhaps, bearing in mind the resurgence of some of the older faiths, now becoming militant − such as the Moslem faith in parts of Asia and west Africa − we may believe that here is one of our last chances of taking the Christian gospel, in its fullness, to these countries.

In Sir Charles Snow's (now Lord Snow's) famous Reith lecture at Cambridge, he spoke of India's needs for trained engineers, where industrialisation calls for between 10 and 20,000 engineers at once. These must be people who 'would shrug off every trace of paternalism . . . people who would muck in as colleagues, who will pass on what they know, do an honest technical job, and get out.' [14] If 20,000 technically-trained Christians went like this, mucked in and passed on what they knew, then, whether or not they got out, they would have done a wonderful job for the Kingdom of Heaven.

There are places where one sees it clearly enough − university students going to teach for less salary than Africans will accept; a doctor friend of mine performing 60 operations every week and running a hospital (which he largely built), for £1,400 a year, and unable to retire because no African doctor will take a lonely job like that with that salary; a regional government education department saying that it would like to get rid of all missionary schools, but is not able to do so, despite strong nationalist feeling, because, although the missionary societies may be limited in what they can do, they do it better and more cheaply than Africans can do it. To see these things is to know that there is a call to thousands in Britain who do not yet respond. At a teachers' training college a little while ago I heard the chaplain talking to the students about the sorts of work that they could do when their training was complete. He turned to the young women in the little circle where I was, and he said: 'You ought not to be saying: "Is there any reason why I should go abroad?" You ought to be saying: "Is there any reason why I should not go?"'

We have come to the core of the problem of responsible action: 'Why should I do it?' Surely, in all these cases, it must be because I have seen something about life. For responsibility is, ultimately, our reply to something which we have seen. In *The Affluent Society*, published a few years ago, Galbraith quoted on the title page a phrase from another economist: 'The economist, like every other person, must be concerned with the ultimate aims of humanity.' Here is part of the tragedy of the trades union movement, which began so clearly to assert these claims, and now seems to have lost its inspiration. Here is the danger in any welfare state − the greatest temptation for any socialist administration. The most important question to ask about anyone is, what are their ultimate aims, what is their inner character; what are they for? We can only plan for other people if we know their true nature, and are prepared sympathetically to enter into it and share it. A report of the World Council of Churches[15] says: 'The question of what it means to be human is one of the most pressing questions involved in all the concrete decisions that have to be taken in the industrial order.' Here technical knowledge, like patriotism, is not enough. It simply is not true, in John Dewey's famous phrase, that 'morality is an engineering issue'. Nor is it true, as a Christian sociologist once said, that 'if 600 scientists working together could produce the atomic bomb, then 600 scientists could deal with the problem of race hatred'. St Paul knew better than that — 'the evil that I would not, that I do'.

So, in the early days when the World Council of Churches was exploring the idea of a responsible society, it could write[16]: 'There is hope for the development of a responsible society where two convictions are held with equal force: first that freedom lacks substance unless it is combined with economic justice and, second, that the quest for economic justice leads to new forms of oppression unless it is united with an insistent concern for political and spiritual freedom.' No one can say what spiritual freedom means unless they can answer our prior question: what does it mean to be a human being? And surely it is here that the Christian has been granted a certain insight — the insight without which scientists will not know how to use their growing control over nature, or government be able to propose and put through the huge legislative programmes of which we have been thinking. The Christian knows that whatever else may be said about a person, we must not forget the most important thing of all — that he or she is a child of God; with the freedom, the privileges, the responsibilities that attach to that family character.

'The making of a good society,' says Lord Beveridge,[17] 'depends not on the state, but on the citizens, acting individually or in free association with one another, acting on motives of various kinds, some selfish, others unselfish, some narrow and material, others inspired by love of people and love of God. The happiness or unhappiness of the society in which we live, depends upon ourselves as citizens, not on the instrument of political power we call the state. Knowledge and reason applied to social conditions by voluntary action have led to a great development of action by the state. This does not end voluntary action or the philanthropic motive. It sets them free for new objectives.'

Some of these new objectives have been mentioned in this lecture. In white papers and government reports they are spelled out repeatedly under the label 'technical assistance'. And in it all, the significance of persons and personal commitment is continually stressed. Thus the Overseas Development Institute pamphlet *Aid to Africa*: 'In general, technical aid, whether in the form of operational staff or of experts, is a higher priority than financial assistance . . . . if we are serious about aid giving, improving the supply of suitable people to work in underdeveloped countries, especially in agriculture and related fields, is a high priority.' And Dr Bilheimer, in *Ethical Problems of Economic Aid and Technical Assistance*: 'An expert of high technical qualifications may be an utter failure if he does not have the right spiritual ones. Obviously no responsible administrator will take a technically second-rate person. Increasingly, however, the demand is for high spiritual qualities as a prerequisite for the effective exercise of their technical capabilities.'[18]

Surely it comes to this, that (in the words of Professor Titmuss) we need 'pioneers in the art of giving' and Christians, of all people, ought to be able to supply that need. It is vastly more important that the Christian community should concern itself with these issues than with some of its perennial topics — the colour and shape of a minister's garment or whether he is to stand at the north or south end of the communion table. If we in the Christian community do not set the pattern of thought and service for the rest of the community, this pattern will be set by others who do not have the magnanimity, or the insight, that God gives. It is, therefore, more important that we be involved in politics than whether our involvement be as Christian socialists, Christian conservatives or Christian liberals. 'The theological question of today is not, "Where is God and how can I know Him?" but, "Where is my neighbour and how do I live with him?" My neighbour is no longer the man that shares my life in the village or who belongs to the same parish. My neighbour is everyone with whom life throws me into contact. And these contacts of dependence go out now to the ends of the earth.'[19]

It is not until a substantial body of men and women have learnt to answer that theological question in an active, experimental fashion that a society can be called responsible. 'Moral advice and the proclamation of moral ideas are insufficient. Only that which transcends morals, namely the knowledge of the ultimate account-ability of people and society to God, and of the Grace of God by which people, being forgiven, forgive one another, can be the foundation of personal responsi-bility and responsible society.'[20]

All this reminds us that the very word 'responsibility' comes from the verb 'respond' − to make a movement towards someone − to react − and in that move-ment to express human solidarity. I think it was Dr F. H. Heinemann who took Descartes' famous phrase, 'Cogito, ergo sum,' and changed it to 'Respondeo, ergo sum.' But Professor Rosenstock-Huessy, worried because the concentration on self implied by the dogmatic 'sum' − I am − at the end seemed to spoil the freedom of the 'respondeo' at the beginning, has changed it to a still better form: 'Respondeo, etsi mutabor' − I respond, even though I shall be changed.[21] Meeting people, liv-ing with them, thinking for them − these will not leave me unchanged. Respon-sibility in this sense has no grain of patronage, as if we, who have been well-treated by Providence, now look down in pity upon those who have not. Rather does it speak of the family of God living the life of the family of God; which is the ultimate basis of true responsibility. It is only that kind of spirit which can save us from making a mess of the various projects that we devise to help the underdeveloped countries; that can enable us sometimes to speak, sometimes to be silent; sometimes to act, sometimes to hesitate. It is that kind of spirit that enables us to be sensitive to the deep traditions of the people among whom we are living, and to whom we are responding, all round the world.

Responsibility is a gift − you can no more will it than you can will freedom. A friend of mine has said that the 'so-called free world is not a place where people are already free: it is a school for those determined to become free'. In the same way we can say of our present topic that our community is a sort of school for those determined to act responsibly, and take the risks of being changed, as we deal with other members of the family of God.

How is it done? There is no prescription for it, no magic ointment for the body politic. In the last resort this kind of responding, which is the basis of all other, can be achieved only by people of goodwill. Often, but by no means always, they will be Christians. Perhaps most of all they will be humble of heart, who know both struggle and victory, because they have experienced these things in their own lives. We are mostly not politicians, or scientists, or leaders of social policy. But we are all children of God. So we share a responsibility, which will show itself in the way we think and talk no less than in the quiet confidence with which, as Christians, we face and then enter the secular world. It is God's world we enter; it is God's command that we obey; and it is God's promise that we discover when, in this deep sense, we are shown what it means to be responsible people.

This lecture was given in February, 1965

References

1 One of the best-known leaders of the Humanist movement in Britain is a member of Christian Action.

2 *Christian Responsibility in One World,* by A. Theodore Eastman, Seaburg Press, New York, 1965.

3 From the report, *The Church and the Disorder of Society*, issued by the World Council of Churches after the Amsterdam general assembly in 1948.

4 An anonymous article in *Student World*, No. 3, 1963.

5 'Trade Aid for "have-nots"', by K. Norsky in *The Guardian*, March 23, 1961.

6 Oxfam *Broadsheet*, January 28, 1965.

7 A valuable handy survey of this and other related matters is in a lecture, *The Needs of Developing Nations*, by Arthur Gaitskell, 1964, published by Oxfam.

8 In *The Science of Science*, ed M. Goldsmith and A. Mackay, London, Souvenir Press 1964.

9 From an interview with Hans Bethe, *Bulletin of Atomic Scientists*, 18, 24, 1962.

10 I have tried to develop this idea further in my *Science, Technology and the Christian*, Epworth Press 1960.

11 A very full account of this episode is by Alice K. Smith, in the *Bulletin of Atomic Scientists*, October 1938.

12 An excellent account is in a report; 'The Integrity of Science', published in the *American Scientist* for June, 1965, and prepared by a committee on science in the promotion of human welfare, associated with the American Association for the Advancement of Science (AAAS).

13 World Council of Churches report at Enugu, Nigeria, January, 1965 — *The Ecumenical Programme for Emergency Action in Africa*.

14 C. P. Snow, *The Two Cultures*, Cambridge University Press, 1959.

15 Arnoldshain conference, 1956.

16 *Christian Action in Society*, I. *The Responsible Society*, issued by the study department of the World Council of Churches, Geneva, 1949.

17 *Voluntary Action*, Allen and Unwin, 1948.

18 For these two quotations I am indebted to the CMS *Newsletter*, January, 1965.

19 T. R. Morton in *The Coracle*, the journal of the Iona Community, March, 1965.

20 Report of the East Asia Christian Conference, Bangkok, December, 1949.

21 See J. H. Oldham in *Question*, 6, 84, 1953;

Donald Soper
Socialism — an enduring creed

Anybody embarking upon a lecture in honour of Tawney would, as a matter of courtesy, preface what he had to say by expressing his sense of honour and privilege in being part of this great succession of lectures. For me it is a profound sense of gratitude that I voice because I can, I think without dishonesty, claim that Tawney did not necessarily convert me to socialism, but he provided for me seminal thoughts and principles about the Christian Socialist Movement which have moulded by thinking ever since and, I daresay, have moulded the thinking of most of you who are here today. He was a truly great man in the economy as well as the profundity of his work and in the continuing influence which I think he bears upon any constructive socialist thinking today. Therefore it is for me, as I repeat a very great privilege to take part in this succession of Tawney lectures. May they be recognised for what Tawney did, and may their virtue consist in the faithfulness with which they represent his spirit and his teaching.

A preliminary word about the title. We live in a world which has comprehended, or at least come to appreciate, the experience of what the Greeks said so long ago: 'Everybody is in a state of change.' Until comparatively recently that change was slow and was a change in degree rather than in kind. No-one, I think, would object to the claim today (of which such contemporary examples as the silicon chip provide evidence) that change has now broken into a gallop, and in many cases the bit is between the teeth of the technological age, and in some respects the horse has bolted. The question therefore arises, for those who would seek a permanent mental and spiritual habitation, whether any house can withstand the contemporary storm or whether all ideologies are not built ultimately upon sand.

I am trying to be a Christian Socialist because I believe that, although I live in a world where change and decay is all around, I tend to see there are those things which persist, and there are those creeds which endure. And against the backcloth of some present-day cynicism and flight from ultimate reason, Tawney, it seems to me, stands not only as a lighthouse but also as a wall impregnable behind which we can take our comfort, from which we can make our assays, and in which we can find our ultimate security.

In the first lecture dedicated to the memory and inspiration of Tawney our friend Stanley Evans selected the theme of equality, and how splendidly he adorned it, and how impoverished has been the movement since his sudden and tragic end. I will not venture upon the path which he took. What I would prefer to do is to select out of the teachings of Tawney two other seminal thoughts and endeavour in some substance to treat them both, and thereafter to apply what seems to me to be the Christian answer to the problems they raise and the perils they infer. Tawney, in addition to his book on equality, wrote two other books which became well known. One of them was *Religion and the Rise of Capitalism* and the other was *The Acquisitve Society*. I believe that any attempt to understand the present trend of things, and at the same time to maintain a faith in the Christian socialist position, requires every more careful attention to the prime propositions belonging to both those very great books. I will some little time in adumbrating the nature of the argument, among others, with which those two volumes at length are concerned. In principle and with profound eloquence, and with a historical background which is, I think, impregnable, Tawney asserted that in the process of the development of the western hemisphere an obligation to the church was lost. Before the rise of capitalism and the corresponding emergence of the nation state, in the days of what we call Christendom, whatever might have been our activities and our sinfulness, at least our affairs had to be referred to the Christian concept and, above all, the Christian ethic. Officially Christianity was regarded as mandatory.

Let me give you three illustrations of that, which show not only the obligation and its relevance, or reference, but also the way in which that reference was to a large extent nullified. The Christian church in the emergence of a money system, even in its primitive forms, was concerned to fulfil the gospel obligation to refrain from usury. Therefore the Christian church proclaimed to all and sundry, whether they went to church or whether they didn't, and most people did, that usury was impermissible. But, of course, with the emergence of any economy with which money was associated, some form of usury was inevitable. The Christian church laid down that, though usury was impermissible, under two conditions it could be tolerated. They both sound rather more impressive in Latin than they would do if you translated them into vulgar tongues. One was that you could take usury if there were a situation of what was called *lucrum cessans*, which meant that you could take usury if, by not taking it, you lost money. You could also take usury if the situation were what was called of *damnum emergens*, which means that you could take usury if it were profoundly to your disadvantage not to take it. Now whether we can, as I think, look with kindly or unkindly contempt on these evasions at least we must remember that our human affairs in a pre-capitalist and pre-capital state era were, by necessity, referred to moral issues springing from what our forefathers imagined to be the Christian creed.

Let me give you another illustration. When Christopher Columbus was looking for the back door to India and found the front door to America, he sketched a map, brought it home and, quite naturally, took it to the Pope. He did not take it to some business enterprise or some cartel. He took it to the Pope and, so we are told (and I am putting it in colloquial language), the Pope looked quite wise about it. He said he had known that America was there all the time but hadn't said anything about it. He then took a pencil out of his pocket and drew a line down the middle of that map. He said all on one side of the line would go to Portugal for the glory of God and all on the other side of the line would go to Spain for the glory of God. He at least believed that whatever new lands were to be discovered, and whatever new conditions were to prevail, it was the business of the church to have the first say. The Spanish conquistadors' subsequent atrocious treatment of their fellow human beings in the Caribbean, the Tainos, was all the more reprehensible since Jesus Christ, their avowed master, taught that all people were equally precious in the sight of God and that all oppression was contrary to His will.

Last year, on holiday in the Dordogne, I went to the very great Beynac Castle. I wonder if you know what happened at Beynac Castle? During the crusades Richard the Lionheart was staying there. He heard that a neighbouring abbot had some money and he thought he could do a better job with it and so he went over to the abbot's castle and claimed the money. An interfering sharpshooter on the roof, thinking he was an enemy, hit him with a crossbow and he died. Immediately his holiness of Rome said that, although shooting with bows and arrows might be compatible with the Christian faith in a just war, the use of crossbows was to be prohibited. Nobody took any notice but nevertheless the church behaved as if it had an inalienable right and responsibility.

Now what Tawney says is that, with the coming of the nation state and with the coming of the early capitalist era, the Christian framework had to be entirely abandoned and another framework of 'so-called' ethics had to take its place. Politically that ethic referred to the nation states emerging at the Reformation and obeying the doctrine of *cujos regio ejus religio*. This meant quite simply that where you had a tract of land and an army, which was itself omnicompetent, that tract of land or that community of people had every right to make up its own religion in order the better to satisfy the needs of that particular group. Ultramontanism was inevitably repudiated and politically every state was necessarily committed to violence because that was the only category which specified what was a state and what wasn't. Every state had its own right to proscribe what religious principles it desired. In many cases, of course, there was a squabble over whether the principles operating from the Vatican were to be preferred or the principles operating from Geneva. Nevertheless it was the first stage in the secularisation of the nation state, and no longer was the question whether or not war was, from a moral standpoint of Christianity, permissible, its justification was entirely within the framework of the interests of the nation state. Even more markedly was the essence of the Christian critique abolished in the economic sphere, as Tawney convincingly demonstrates, in the primitive and developing economies consequent very largely upon the discovery of silver, the emancipation of the mediaeval serf and the emergence of the middleman. Another kind of ethic (if you call it an ethic) more suitable to the interests of this emergent nationalism and emergent capitalism took its place.

The question which I think lies at the heart of what I want to say to you is this: what has happened since?

Tawney demonstrated this truth as having an all-important relevance to the question of society today and requiring, as he of course believed, and I do, a socialist community. What has happened I can put best, I think, in the language of people like Arthur Koestler. Arthur Koestler is variously regarded — some people think of him as a polymath and others as a man educated rather above his intelligence. Well, you can take your view, whichever you like, but I think you disagree with him at your peril. What he says is simply this: the prime characteristic of a secular state is its violence, and that characteristic of capitalism which is its violence can now be represented as a fatal flaw, not only in certain states and among certain groups, but also a fatal flaw of the human species itself. It is exaggerated and compounded by the kind of situations, political and economic, in which we now find ourselves, having rejected the moral obligations of the Christian faith and, indeed, all moral obligations which stand over against the prosecution of particular ends and purposes as represented alike by the nation state and the capitalist system. To quote Arthur Koestler, if you ask why did the brontosaurus have its day and pass away — there aren't any left — why did the sabre-tooth tiger disappear, why has the mammoth disappeared, the answer is because there were flaws in their make-up which were incompatible with the challenges and conditions under which they came to live.

Arthur Koestler says the failures in the make-up of human beings are unique, particularly in the realm of violence. For instance a swarm of locusts will devour almost anything except another swarm of locusts but people devour themselves with their armies, with their nuclear bombs, with their organised violence. Moreover, if you look at the correspondence columns of the daily press over the past few weeks, particularly after the Afghanistan crisis, you will, I think, be prepared to agree with me that we are now hearing once again the vocabulary of violence, indeed its inevitability. Instead of contemplating what we can do to prevent the next war we are becoming accustomed and brainwashed to think of something we can do when it has happened, as if there will still be, even if there isn't a fence at the top of the cliff, an ambulance at the bottom. I don't believe there will be. I think it will be a hearse.

We have now, it seems to me, reached a quite terminal point in human violence. I won't elaborate it because I think most of you are aware of it but it makes the relevance of the Tawney argument all the more imperative. We are now at last — at long last — confronted with the fruition of this evil tree that could never have grown and borne its wicked fruit had it not been for the abandonment of those overall moral principles which said, 'thus far and no further', whatever the circumstances. I am a committed and absolute pacifist in intention because I believe there is no way of domesticating or civilising war; rather do I believe that this is a terminal condition which may obliterate the human species and not merely be a very dreadful holocaust from which the majority of people will survive.

That is one of the elements in the contemporary scene which I believe demands the recognition of the enduring creedal statement of Christian socialism seen against the backcloth of this analysis by Tawney.

Now I turn to the other one. It is found in the book which he wrote called *The Acquisitive Society*. It is in that book that he adumbrates the process whereby we are increasingly encouraged to think in terms of what we can get and what we can accumulate and what we can acquire. There are two profoundly important reasons why this takes its place in the behaviour pattern of human, sinful, creatures like we are. It didn't happen to any great extent for some of our forefathers because they had no large-scale opportunity of acquisitiveness. I wonder to what an extent we have appreciated the profound difference in the attitude, shall we say, of an Indian peasant or, indeed, other peasants three or four hundred years ago, to a world in which there was practically no chance of them acquiring anything very much except the will to go on living until they were about 40. It should surprise nobody that in that context the church proclaimed the primacy of making a good death rather than living a good life because, in terms of acquirement of amenities, a good life was out of the question for most people. May I remind you that for most people it still is.

Now what has happened, as Tawney pinpoints, is that, over a period of not much more than 150 years, the rate of change in the acquisitive capacity of the human race has enormously increased. It has increased a thousand fold over the previous opportunities for acquisition belonging to an age in which, after the decay of the Roman empire, acquisitiveness in a very large degree declined because the opportunities for it in the dark ages were even more severely minimised. But what happens when this opportunity prevails? You can see it very clearly in what we call the capitalist system and in the thinking of the Conservative Party, where they think! You can quote the authority Lord Hailsham who, in his paperback on *The Nature of Conservatism*, asserts that it is built on the principle of self-interest.

Enlightened self-interest, theologically, is only a baptismal word for selfishness. Enlightened self-interest for our parents was the prospect of bliss beyond this earth, whereas enlightened self-interest for the contemporary generation, even in times of depression, means an ever greater opportunity, by foul means or fair, to acquire those things which belong to the amenities and the pleasures of life. I hasten to remind myself of those valuable and prophetic words of Jesus, that people's lives consisteth not in the abundance of the things that they possess. Do not build up treasures on earth where moth and rust corrupt and where thieves break through and steal but lay up for yourselves treasures in the heavenly places, for where your treasure is there will your heart be also.

Here the Marxist is far nearer the truth than some evangelical professors of the Christian faith. Marx asserts, or rather he was the populariser of what was in the process of being asserted by a great many other people, that when people get the opportunity of selfishness they are very likely to respond to it and, as they respond, so do they progressively find eroded in themselves the concepts of comradeship and fellowship and cooperation and peace. Whatever may be our particular and immediate concepts of the processes as they will develop over the next few years, surely Tawney was equally, and equally profoundly, right, in asserting that, in the present condition of technological and scientific revolution, the emphasis will still be on acquisitiveness as the be-all and *summum bonum*. This will be so unless we are persuaded by other means and from other motives to reject that kind of acquisitiveness in the interests of the common good. What was said in *The Acquisitive Society* is an enduring fact, magnified in many respects as is the violence involved in the contentions about relgion and the capitalist society, and it is only insofar as we take on board the significance of these two enduring factors that we can persist in our belief in the endurance of that creed which alone can outpace them and outdo them.

I would like to take a minute or two to be a little melancholy. Not that I enjoy being melancholy, and I hope to recover, but because I think that one of the things that we are inclined to ignore in Tawney, unless we take him sufficiently seriously, is his great appreciation of the fact of evil. One of the most lamentable effects of the decay of religious faith is that the modern generation in very large part has lost its sense of appropriate guilt. It has lost its sense of personal sinfulness. I remember an afternoon in Hyde Park when a man in the crowd said he had never committed a sin. I understand he was the only member of his family present when he made the observation, but he made it and he gained a certain amount of approval on the proposition that the speaker, myself, would not be able to define sin. Well, I cannot define love but I know what it is all about, and I cannot define sin, in complete terms, but I know what it is about and, I am sure, it is the second strongest thing in the universe. Furthermore, if people today imagine that we can understand these two seminal concepts of Tawney and operate a socialist Christian kind of ideology, so as to rid ourselves of the menace of sinfulness, then that is cloud cuckoo land. Morality is not necessarily the product of ideology.

No one can doubt that, if you have to compare the ultimate value of socialism with the ultimate value of Christianity, Christianity must come first. That is not something I say because I am wearing a clerical collar, it is something which I believe is basically true. Ultimately we are moral beings or immoral beings and the question of morality must take precedence over the question of political suitability. That is another way of saying that what is morally right can never be politically wrong. It is also a way of saying that nothing is politically satisfactory unless it is geared to a moral proposition which is irrefutable.

I invite you to look once more at these two propositions of Tawney. Look at them in the light of the faith which brings us together today and in the light of prospects that lie ahead. I have no confidence in that kind of argument much-publicised today that if only you get enough people interested in the real issues they will almost automatically respond in the right way to them. That is what was said to me when I was a very young man, that if you could really get people interested in religion they would agree to it. My experience is that, quite often, getting an interest in religion provides rather better reasons for not believing it until that interest becomes deepened. Christianity asserts that, before you can operate even that which is reasonably true and morally desirable, you must secure a greater authority than can merely be mobilised out of your own resources. I make no bones about asserting, as Tawney himself asserted time and time again, that by grace are we saved through faith and not of ourselves; it is the gift of God.

I have spent a good deal of time in this Christian Socialist Movement and I have heard many enlightened and interesting debates on what we should do about the Labour Party. We haven't made up our minds yet, I hope. I have heard many a discussion on the political issues of the day. I feel that we should have spent more time on asking ourselves where we were going to get the power to put into effect those things which we would like to see. I have no doubt that the first requirement, if we are to reduce the peril of war — and it can only finally be obliterated by complete disarmament — is to be prepared to reduce our own acquisitiveness to the point where the full life is not coterminus with the acquisition of amenities. Only in so doing do I believe that the future offers any hope whatsoever.

I am not arguing, as I have said many times in the open air, that you can't get to heaven unless you are a Methodist, and that you can't get the Christian Socialist Movement going unless you are a Methodist. On the other hand I am not asking anybody to take undue risks; what I am saying is that, unless you have a faith which goes beyond the calculation of effects as represented by recognisable ingredients in a contemporary situation, there is no hope of the emergence of that peaceful community. Therefore, quite sincerely, I believe that a pilgrimage to the foot of the cross is the prerequisite of any hope that we can learn from the teachings of people like Tawney and apply them to the resolution of our present problems in the light of what we believe to be Christian socialism.

Having said that I would finish with something rather different or, rather, not different but consequential. I have referred to the requirement of total disarmament. I cannot avoid the conclusion that the teaching of the cross requires such total disarmament and I would not harass you now with arguments with which you are probably very familiar. Rather I would put it in a nutshell, if I may, by saying, supposing it is a tremendous hazard, is it not true, on the basis of comparative risk, when we have committed ourselves to the risk of war, time and time again in the acquisitive and capitalist society and in the nation state, we have known that in our committal we could not rely on the Christian ethic or the Christian promise for it had been abandoned? If that is so, is there not a call which should be issued with clarion precision that we should at least demonstrate the value of taking comparable risks for peace? These may bring with them great difficulties and hardships and suffering but, as we confidently believe, those risks are not just taken out of the blue. They are part of the profound and ultimate intention of God our Heavenly Father. If it is a faith then, in God's name, let us take that risk. That is what I believe the Christian socialist has to say with regard to the manifestion of violence in the contemporary society.

Lastly, what have Christian socialists to say when they have made their pilgrimage to the foot of the cross? What have they to say to the companion problem of a selfish human society or a selfish human species which has been perverted and adulterated by the acquisitive capacity which science and technology have thrown into our laps? It seems to me the only answer is that which extends to the Christian concept of the family, which is the basis of Christian socialism, and applies it to the whole world. Only insofar as we are prepared to deny ourselves for the good of others can we produce a contrary principle sufficient to deny the worst effects of acquisitiveness. What the Christian socialist, it seems to me, has to do today is to demonstrate that true happiness and true fulfilment of life are not coterminous with the accumulation of gadgets or the benefactions of technology.

The only life that is really worth living is the caring life. That is not just a pious aspiration. It is the logic of the very world in which either we seek that intelligent way of comradeship or we commit ourselves irretrievably to a computerised death; and there is no intention to end this lecture with some kind of large and provocative statement. I believe that the apocalyptic concept that has so often been found in Christian thinking is the only true concept which is appropriate for today. I do not believe in the vast and almost unlimited extension of this world's affairs from which we may stumble from disaster to greater disaster but it will all go on. I believe that the apocalyptic message is that we are at least within shouting and shooting distance of the end of the age. I wonder whether the Christian church and the socialist movement will be able to command first the faith and then the perception to make other people realise, as they come to realise it themselves, that a rebirth of the human race in non-violence and social care is necessary. That is the one answer which is approved of God, sanctified at the cross and verified in the resurrection morning. Faith, if it is realised, can, within movements such as this, be the bell-wether of good news and a gospel for all mankind.

This lecture was given in March, 1980.

Frank Field
Socialism and the politics of radical redistribution

This lecture is concerned with the political implications of a no-growth economy as it impinges upon an increasing army of poor people, and with the possibilities of radical forms of redistribution. This is a central theme of Tawney's work, and one to which he addressed himself during the inter-war years.

If the high rates of economic growth in the 1950s and early 1960s laid the basis for post-war consensus politics, it is the Yom Kippur War, the resulting slow-down in the world economy and the particularly marked change in the British economy, which has ushered in a new political era. Apart from the necessity of policies to stimulate the economy, the left must extend the discussion beyond questions of spending and creating new wealth to how best to redistribute existing wealth and income. This transition is essential if truly radical politics are to be pursued. This is the lecture's first theme. But a fundamental reorientation of British politics is called for on other grounds too. Post-war consensus politics has still left British society with marked class differences as well as a growing number of poor. These are the issues explored in the second section of the lecture. The third theme concerns the politics of redistribution. This will entail not only a redistribution from rich to poor, from men to women, but also spreading the earnings from up to 40 years of work over a lifetime of 80 years, as well as a significant redistribution from the state to individual.

Whether any of these changes are possible without a new sense of moral purposefulness is open to doubt. The importance of Tawney's contribution to this aspect of today's debate is the final theme of a lecture celebrating Tawney's contribution to Christian socialism.

The end of post-war consensus

Central to the post-war political consensus has been a set of beliefs stemming from the role performed by economic growth and, as on so many issues, the clearest exponent was Anthony Crosland. Crosland believed growth provided the formula for leaving the rich rich, while also lessening the poverty of the poor. Writing after the 1970 election defeat Crosland began with a frank admission: 'I was too complacent about growth in the *Future of Socialism*'. [1] He listed the objectives to which Labour was still committed: the abolition of poverty, massive increases in public spending on education, housing and health, as well as mounting a major attack on environmental pollution. He continued his argument by adding, 'Certainly we cannot even approach our basic objectives with the present state of growth. For

49

these objectives . . . require a redistribution of resources; and we shall not get this unless our total resources are growing rapidly'.

By developing this theme Crosland expressed one of the key premises of post-war consensus politics. 'I do not of course mean that rapid growth will automatically produce a transfer of resources of the kind we want; whether it does or not will depend on the social and political values of the country concerned. But *I do assert dogmatically that in a democracy low or zero growth wholly excludes the possibility*. For a substantial transfer then involves not only a relative but an absolute decline in real incomes of the better off half of the population . . . and this they will frustrate'. (emphasis added)

Crosland concluded by saying that in a utopia, or a dictatorship, it might be possible to transfer resources of a near or static GNP to the have-nots but, 'In the rough democratic world in which we live, we cannot.'

Many more people are now aware that the current recession is different from previous swings in economic activity. Unemployment is higher than at any time during the past 35 years and at present the government does not hold out the prospect of returning to full employment. And while much time is spent puzzling over the economic indicators, little or no time is given to plotting the political consequences to our society of the loss of an ever rising national income.

One reason why we are so unprepared is that the scenarios presented by the revisionists excluded consideration of the world in which we now find ourselves. Crosland's argument was nothing if not comforting. Radicalism could be put on ice while awaiting a return to a high level of economic activity. The one possibility which was not discussed by Crosland, or subsequently by any of his disciples, was that a period of slow growth could result in real cuts in the living standards of the poor. But this is the future we now face. Powerful forces are at work increasing the numbers of poor. Slow growth will increase the numbers made poor by unemployment and demographic changes are adding daily to the welfare rolls. Real cuts in the poor's standard of living will occur if the current period of slow growth is not accompanied by a redistribution of existing income to the poor.

The first challenge comes from the ever growing dole queues. Today the unemployed number 2.5 million and the latest estimate from the department of employment projects a rise in the labour force of a million by 1986. On a conventional assumption about productivity (an increase of 2 per cent per annum) it is estimated that a growth rate approaching 3 per cent per annum would be required to stabilise, let alone reduce, the current record post-war level of unemployment.

It is on the basis of a growth rate below the level required to match the expected increase in the labour supply and productivity, together with the government's deflationary policies, that all forecasting organisations project a rise in the numbers of the unemployed. It has been assumed here that the 1.8 million unemployed in 1980 will double by 1985. Increasing unemployment will affect the amount spent on the social security budget in two ways. In the first place more claims will be made on the insurance benefits scheme as a greater number of people draw unemployment benefit. Secondly, larger numbers of the unemployed will also be drawing supplementary benefit.

At a time when the numbers of unemployed are likely to increase, demographic changes are taking place which will also increase the number of households on low income. The major change on this front is the increase in the numbers of single parent families. Recently the number of one parent families has been increasing by 60,000 a year (around 6 per cent). If this rate of increase is maintained over the next five years the number of one parent families will grow from a total of 920,000 in 1980 to 1,220,000 by 1985. This increase in the number of one parent families will have a major effect on the social security budget. At the present time 30 to 40 per cent of one parent families depend on supplementary benefit. If the same ratio is maintained we can estimate that by 1985 there will be 425,000 single parent families drawing supplementary benefit.

In making estimates about the future size of the social security budget, another group that must be taken into account is of retirement pensioners. Although the number of retirement pensioners will not increase greatly in the next five or 10 years (their numbers will in fact have declined by the turn of the century) expenditure on retirement pensions and supplementary pensions now accounts for more than 50 per cent of the total social security budget.

If the living standards of the old and the poor are to be maintained at a time when the number made poor by unemployment, as well as the numbers of one parent families in poverty, are growing, the social security budget for these three groups will need to rise from £14,700 million in 1980–81 to £20,325 million by 1985 (1980–81 prices). For this sum to be achieved without any redistribution will require a growth rate of 3.6 per cent over each of the years up to 1985. On the evidence so far available this looks highly unlikely. Indeed, in the year up to the third quarter of 1980, GDP *fell* by 5.5 per cent.

The product of growth

If, as I have suggested, a future based on no growth means increasing numbers of poor people, and increasing relative poverty, is the converse true? Does growth automatically guarantee the erosion or elimination of poverty? Recent history suggests otherwise. The post-war boom resulted in a significant rise in the living standards of all groups of the population. But although national income grew at an almost unprecedented rate in many areas, life chances between classes remained stubbornly the same and the rise in prosperity has not resulted in a comprehensive narrowing of the gap between the living standards of the poor and the rest of the community. Indeed, during this period the numbers of poor increased significantly.

In 1948 around a million households were dependent on supplementary benefits (NA/SB taken as a definition of poverty). The latest figures show that today a few more than three million households are dependent on supplementary benefits. If we count the number of dependents, rather than the number of households, living on supplementary benefit, the total rises to more than five million. There are, in addition, more than two and a half million people living on incomes below the supplementary benefit poverty line.

The years of growth saw an increase in the numbers of poor, and this increase cannot be accounted for totally by the use of a more generous definition of poverty. And it is stressed that this increase in poverty occurred during an unprecedented period of growth. A rising national income does not automatically eliminate poverty in advanced industrial countries. Had the post-war boom continued into the eighties and on into the nineties, the rise in the numbers of people on low incomes would itself have been grounds for questioning the basis of consensus politics.

A growing national income failed radical politics on another score. Despite the rising living standards for practically all groups of the population, this rise in prosperity has left significant class differences in life chances between different groups of the population and in some instances these have widened during the post-war period. There are two reasons why the early period during life is important to the argument developed here. In the first place it is the time when the effect of the environment can most clearly be seen, for we are at our most vulnerable. The period is also important because if we exclude miscarriages in early pregnancy, death is now most frequent in the last stage of pregnancy up until the first birthday, and while the number of deaths during this period continues to fall, more lives are lost during this 15 month period than during the next 25 years.

A commonly accepted view is that rising prosperity will, of its own volition, abate class inequalities. In particular there was, and to some extent still is, the belief that a steadily rising national income, together with the introduction of the National Health Service, would wipe out class differences. Research over a period of 20 years has confounded this optimism.[2]

During the post-war period there have been three major, bench mark, studies of children born during one week. These took place in 1946, 1958 and 1970. The first was by J. W. B. Douglas, who looked at all confinements in Great Britain during the first week of March 1946. He noted that there were considerable social class differences in deaths during the first month of life, and showed that approximately half of the deaths were of premature infants (childrenn weighing less than 5½ lbs at birth). Dr Douglas then considered which mothers were most likely to give birth to premature babies and concluded: 'Prematurity was least common in the most prosperous groups; 4.2 per cent of the children of professional and salaried workers were premature as compared with 6.5 per cent of black-coated workers, 6.7 per cent of manual workers and 7.2 per cent of agricultural workers.'[3]

The second major perinatal mortality survey was carried out in 1958 on 17,000 children. The results were similar to Dr Douglas's in the differences in infant mortality rates according to social class. Among the 17,000 children it was found: 'There is a rise from a mortality ratio of 69 in social class 1 to 128 in social class 5. With unmarried mothers the mortality rate for the foetus was even higher at 140 per 1,000 births'.[4]

The third major study was of all births during one week in 1970. Reporting on the perinatal rates the survey found that these rose from 7.5 for social class 1 to 27.6 for babies born to mothers in social class 5 and 37.4 for single mothers. In accounting for these differences, Roma Chamberlain reported one reason why social class 1 mothers recorded such low perinatal mortality was that a greater proportion of the missing cases and unmatched deaths should be allotted to this class. Even so, the rate for social class 2 is not much more than half of that of social class 5 and the study concluded that, 'there is nothing to contradict and everything to support the theory that social class differences are widening rather than diminishing.'[5]

At the end of 1976, the committee enquiring into child health services published its report and one of its findings summarises the argument presented here. *Fit for the Future* recorded that, 'twice as many children of unskilled workers die in the first month of life as children of professional workers *and the gap between the social classes in this respect has widened steadily for 25 years*'.[6] Those were the years of unprecedented prosperity for this country. So much then for the supposed automatic levelling effect of economic growth.

Radical redistribution

It is against this background — of falling national income, threats to the living standards of the poor, an increase in the numbers of the poor, and the continuance of major class differences — that we must look at the forms of redistribution which the next Labour government should take. There will need to be a redistribution not only from rich to poor, but a significant redistribution from men to women, a redistribution which aims to spread the income from work over the income needs of a lifetime, as well as redistribution of cash from the state to the individual.

Arguments for a vertical redistribution of income from rich to poor are sometimes met by scepticism because, even if an aggressive policy of redistribution were followed, few resources would be gained to redistribute to poorer sections of the community. This negative reaction ducks the moral question on whether a redistribution should take place irrespective of the effects of such a policy on the living standards of the poor. It also distracts attention from a key consideration, that is the shares of income taken in tax during the past couple of decades. Since the late 1940s there has been a sharp decline in the proportion of total revenue raised from the rich and less than a third of the fall in the proportion of tax revenue paid by top income groups can be accounted for by a fall of the top 10 per cent share of income.[7] Consequently the tax burden has been rising for other groups and has risen fast for low income groups.

The distributional impact of the Thatcher budgets needs to be viewed against this back-cloth. Despite the evidence of a significant shift in the burden of taxation — vertically onto lower income groups and horizontally onto taxpayers with children — the 1979 budget brought about a major vertical redistribution of income to the rich. The richest 1 per cent of taxpayers cornered 15 per cent of all tax cuts and the richest 7 per cent picked up 34 per cent of the £4.5 billion cut in direct taxation — a total of £1,560 million. The 1980 budget continued this redistribution from those on low incomes to those at the top of the income scale. Although the tax cuts were more modest than the 1979 budget, it was the rich who benefited most. The top 2 per cent of taxpayers gained 14 per cent of all the 1980 tax cuts.

One of the first actions of the next Labour government should be to reverse the tax concessions made to high income groups in the first two budgets of the Thatcher administration. But for socialists and radicals, the politics of a no-growth economy determine that the redistribution has to go beyond what is normally meant by vertical redistribution from rich to poor. It is not just a matter of increasing the rate of tax but of bringing into the tax net income which up to now has been legitimately excluded. This naturally takes discussion onto one of the other four welfare states which operate alongside the traditional welfare state.[8]

At present less than 50 per cent of personal income is taxed. Most is legitimately exempt by one or other of a whole range of tax benefits. These benefits divide neatly into two kinds, those related to the status of the taxpayer and those which are gained as a result of expenditure by the taxpayer. In the first category come the personal allowances which exempt almost £16 billion of personal income from tax. In the second category is the granting of mortgage interest relief (now costing around £2 billion), the massive tax relief to companies (approaching £7 billion), stamp duty exemptions (£1.6 billion), and the exemption of owner-occupied houses from the capital gains tax (estimated at £2.4 billion a year).

The personal tax benefits are justified on the following grounds. One of the cardinal principles of British taxation is that the poor should be exempt from tax and the personal allowances determine what the tax threshold is (ie the point at which a person begins to pay tax). Their other alleged advantage is that they introduce a system of gradation into the tax system.

The allowance system is a very expensive way of failing to achieve this first objective. At the present time the tax threshold is below the supplementary benefit poverty line and the eligibility for the family income supplement. This results in the injustice of the poor paying tax, and the absurd position of many of the poor being given benefit under the family income supplement scheme because their income is so low, but losing most or all of this benefit by way of contribution to the Inland Revenue.

Personal tax benefits are a very crude and expensive way of determining the tax threshold. Each pound of tax benefits not only the poor but also is allotted to those on higher income. And the higher the person's income the higher the value of each pound in allowance is, as the tax benefit is set against the taxpayer's marginal rate of tax. The cost of raising the tax threshold to keep in line with inflation was illustrated in this year's budget. To maintain the tax threshold in real terms would cost the exchequer £2.5 billion. Of this £2.5 billion only 6 per cent would have been of direct benefit to the poor by preventing them moving into the tax net.

The incidence of these tax benefits are highly regressive. The higher the income of the taxpayer the larger the tax benefit he gains. The value of the personal allowances is twice the amount to high income earners as to those near the bottom of the income pile. The impact of the non-personal allowances favours the rich to an even greater extent. In 1979–80, for example, those earning in excess of £10,000 a year made up less than 9 per cent of all taxpayers but they gained 34 per cent of all the mortgage interest tax benefit.

The current public expenditure white paper lists almost 100 tax benefits. Excluding personal allowances, four of the more important benefits for which information is known over the past few years are mortgage interest relief, relief on life assurance premiums, penions schemes and retirement annuity relief for the self employed. In 1975–76, the cost of mortgage interest relief was £805 million. By 1980–81 this had risen to £1,960 million. Over the same period the cost in lost revenue by granting relief on life assurance premiums similarly jumped – from £190 million to £540 million. The cost of granting tax benefit status for pension schemes grew from £400 million to £700 million and pension relief for the self-employed rose from £50 million to £135 million over the same five years.

It would be wrong to wipe out overnight these and other similar personal tax benefits. Expectations and, more importantly, long-term commitments have been entered into on the basis of their existence. However, support could be gained for a three-stage reform developed along the following lines.

The first move in reforming the tax benefit welfare state is to allow what are called the non-personal tax allowances at only the standard rate of tax. The second move is to put a cash ceiling on these non-personal tax benefits. Such a policy would work in the following way. Currently £2 billion is paid out by way of mortgage interest tax relief. It would be unjust to wipe out this relief overnight. But a cash ceiling could be applied at the current level and this sum (£2 billion) be spread over a growing number of owner-occupiers in succeeding years.

Had this been Labour's approach in the 1974 elections and had it had been implemented in its first full year of office (1975–76) the additional reveneue from applying a policy of cash ceilings to just four of the non-personal tax benefits would have been very considerable as the table below shows. In 1980–81 the savings resulting on a cash ceiling imposed in 1975–76 on just these four tax benefits would have resulted in £1,095 million for mortage interest relief, £350 million for life assurance premiums, £300 million for pension schemes and £85 million from the relief in retirement annuities for the self-employed – a total of £1,830 million.

Table: Savings on selected tax benefits by applying a cash ceiling 1975–76 (£ millions)

	1976–77	1977–78	1978–79	1979–80	1980–81	Total
Life assurance premiums	35	45	70	240	350	740
Mortgage interest relief	225	175	245	585	1,095	2,325
Pension schemes	40	30	50	150	300	570
Retirement annuity relief for the self employed	10	15	20	60	85	190

The third readjustment will take longer to implement and shoud be discussed in greater detail. It is to revert back to the exemption system which operated in the income tax system up to 1920. Before this the whole system of tax benefits was of value only to those whose income was below a certain level. Once a taxpayer's income passed beyond this point the whole of the income became eligible for tax. The drawback of this kind of readjustment is obvious. As a person's income crosses the tax threshold a huge poverty trap is created as his or her entire income is then subjected to the first band of tax. It is therefore important to design a vanishing exemption limit whereby the exemption is phased out over a large band of income.

The effect of introducing this change is enormous. The amount of revenue accruing to the exchequer is increased dramatically. *The Economist*, for example, estimated that if all tax benefits were abolished (which is not being advocated here) then the standard rate of tax would be reduced to 15p in the pound. *A policy of curtailing the tax benefit welfare state has the double advantage of increasing the resources for implementing a socialist programme and giving the government scope to reduce rates of tax.*

While discussions on a modified exemption system are proceeding it will be important to debate how best to spread the earnings from work over a lifetime of 80 or more years. For most people the two most vulnerable periods in life are when they are repsonsible for children and when they are old. Women are also put in a vulnerable position when they are responsible for children.[9] Yet the status of married women draws a subsidy which is paid through the husband's wage or salary cheque throughout his working life. The married man's tax allowance currently costs £7 billion in lost revenue. Instead of giving this subsidy spread out through the working life of the husband, it could be paid as a cash benefit to households with young children. If the married man's tax allowance were replaced and the man allowed to claim a single allowance while the wife's earned income relief provision continued, the extra revenue gained would finance a home responsibility payment of £21 a week for each household with children under five, or an allowance of £17 a week for each child under five. The abolition of tax allowance is not advocated here, but a cash ceiling on the married man's tax allowance would result in this benefit being introduced over time. If this reform had been reintroduced in 1975–76 the home responsibility payment would today stand at £10.50 a week for each child under five.

These tax changes will allow a future Labour government to establish a national minimum while at the same time cutting the rate of tax. Crucial to the establishment of a national minimum will be a generous system of child benefits. Child benefits will have a number of roles in helping to create a form of home-made socialism. They are one way of spreading a person's income from work in a way which matches their family responsibilities. They are also an agent for redistributing cash from those on higher incomes to those on lower incomes. A generous system of child benefits also begins to unravel some of the complex problems facing today's welfare state.

Because child benefits are tax free they act as an income floor on which people can build by their own efforts. Many welfare benefits, because they are means tested, act in the opposite way, almost as a ceiling trapping people into poverty. Again, because child benefits are tax free and kept by the family but deducted from benefit when out of work, the larger the family's net income when they are at work than when they are unemployed.

Given the relatively low wages paid to many workers, significant numbers of unemployed find themselves only marginally better off — if at all — by taking a job when one is available. Similarly, once in work, they find it difficult to raise their net income by working overtime, winning a substantial wage increase or by changing their job. The overlap of tax and means tested benefit for families with children now spans such a wide range of incomes that the net spending power of families is about the same (hovering between £64 and £72 a week) irrespective of whether they are earning a weekly wage of £45 or £105.[10] A generous system of child benefits not only blasts the low paid through this poverty trap but also allows reformers to begin campaigning for other welfare changes — such as the introduction of a single parent family allowance — which are non-starters in the absence of a fully developed system of financial support for all children.

Tawney's contribution

British politics is entering into uncharted territory. The end of growth — at least for the forseeable future — has brought to a close the postwar consensus. In a period when rising national income allowed the rich to remain rich, while paying for a programme of social reform, the application of a clear set of moral principles to political behaviour was thought by many people to be less than urgent, if not irrelevant. Today, hard choices have to be made. Politicians and the electorate need to make these choices within a framework of clearly stated values. On this issue, possibly as never before, Tawney's approach is crucially relevant.

Tawney's life and work has two lessons for Labour politics in the 1980s and 1990s. Above everything else Tawney believed that every action, both private and public, should be governed by Christian principles. For him, like Gore, the writ of Christianity was to know no boundaries. The relevance of Christianity applied not just to the personal lives of individuals, but also to their actions as members of society. Personal actions, whether private or public, were to be governed by Christian morality, and each of our activities was seen as but a rung in a ladder stretching from hell to eternity.

Tawney also believed that political beliefs and values had to be lived in people's own everyday lives. As the *New Statesman* commented at the time of Tawney's death: 'The greatness of R. H. Tawney lay in the fact that his life, even more than his work, was his testament.' [11] Tawney more than other socialists this century believed that the good society could be built only by people who were themselves good and who showed this goodness in their daily actions. This side of Tawney's teaching has obvious relevance to the position in which the Labour Party finds itself. The debate in the Labour Party at the present time is dominated by those whose overwhelming emphasis is on changing the structure of society, while leaving unmentioned the crucial importance of individuals changing their attitudes, beliefs and above all their actions. It is almost as if the hard left believes Mrs Thatcher will concede to the Labour Party at the next election and that, once in office and implementing its programme, people will see the obvious justice and fairness of Labour's reforms.

I believe this to be profoundly mistaken. To be built, a successful revolution requires willing participants. Moreover, the nature of the revolution is different if the transformation is brought about, in part at least, by changes in people's attitudes and beliefs. A revolution built from the grass roots is not only one which is likely to be more securely based, but also one which will be improved and strengthened by the people's participation.

Let me end with a further quotation, for it sums up the change in people's hearts which will be required to support the fiscal changes described in this paper, let alone the entire radical transformation upon which the next Labour government must embark: 'Tawney, above all, embodied the vital, but elusive, element that has always distinguished the broad stream of British radicalism from the sectarian doctrines of European socialism — the belief that morality is superior to dogma and that the quality of people's lives matters more than their material achievements. For it is this, fundamentally, that is the common ground for all members of the Labour Party, that provides the touchstone of a person's integrity and marks the dividing line between the levelling democrat and the power-obsessed totalitarian. Tawney never believed in the inevitable triumph of socialism: for him humanism was an act of will, not of history.'[12]

This lecture was given in March, 1981.

1 Crosland, Anthony, *A Social Democratic Britain*, Fabian Society, 1971, pp 2-3.

2 Morris, J. N. and Heady, J. A., 'Social and biological factors in infant mortality', *Lancet*, 12 February 1955.

3 Douglas, J. W. B., *Maternity in Great Britain*, Oxford, 1948.

4 Butler, N. R., and Bonham, D. G., *Perinatal Problems*, Livingstone, 1963.

5 Chamberlain, Roma, *British Births 1970*, Vol 1, Heinemann, 1975.

6 *The Report of the Committee on Child Health Services*, Cmnd 6684, HMSO, 1976.

7 For full argument see Field, Frank, *Inequality in Britain*, Fontana, 1981, pp 109-12.

8 Fully developed in ibid, chapters 7-10.

9 This is not an argument that women rather than men should look after young children, rather a statement of what usually happens.

10 Howell, Ralph, *Why work?*, Conservative Political Centre, 1981.

11 'A Man for All Seasons', *New Statesman*, 19 January 1962.

12 ibid.

Kenneth Leech
Religion and the rise of racism

'Racism dies in order that capital might survive'[1]. So wrote the black radical A. Sivanandan at the conclusion of a review of the development of race legislation and attitudes in Britain in the 1960s and 70s. As immigration control reduced non-white immigrants to a trickle, so race relations legislation sought to curb the incidence of racism within Britain in the interests of state stability. The theory was that, while in terms of immigration policy black people were to be considered merely as labour units, those who managed to beat the controls and settle here were to be seen as equal citizens. Racism at the doors of Britain was seen as necessary to inter-racial harmony inside Britain. However, since then, the fatal flaws in the theory have come to seem increasingly irrelevant as Thatcherism has ushered in an era more obviously hostile both to racial and social justice. Today Sivanandan's words seem excessively optimistic. In the aftermath of the Nationality Bill, the conflicts in Brixton, Liverpool and elsewhere and the government's response to them, the breaking up of family life through immigration rules, and the general lack of interest in government circles in any sustained attack on racial disadvantage, reports of the death of racism can be seen only as exaggerated rumours. The evidence, both internally and internationally, point to the persistence of racism as an integral dimension within capitalism.

In view of this, it is surprising that while Christian social thinkers continue to develop the debate initiated by Max Weber[2] and developed by Tawney[3] on the relationship between religion and capitalism, the study by Ronald Preston[4] being the latest contribution, little attention has been paid to one aspect of the relationship which is of crucial importance for the future of both: the role of religion in aiding and abetting the rise of racism. I want in the lecture therefore to discuss the growth, persistance and spread of racism in our society, its connections with, and implications for, organised Christianity, and the relevance of Tawney's thinking to this discussion.

However, if the neglect of discussion of racism in the English Christian social tradition is striking, its almost total absence from Tawney's work is even more so. As far as I can see, Tawney nowhere wrote about race or racism, except indirectly in his two studies of China[5]. From one perspective, there is perhaps nothing very surprising about this. The concern within the labour movement with race, colonialism and racial justice questions is, for the most part, a post-war phenomenon. The word 'racism' did not enter common vocabulary until the end of the 1960s. The Fabians in particular gave scant attention to colonial issues. Some of the early material such as Bernard Shaw's *Fabianism and the Empire* was appalling. As late as 1949 it is interesting to see the topics which the Fabian Society's conference did not get round to discussing: they were international trade, colonial development, foreign policy and Commonwealth relations![6]

In other respects Tawney's silence on race is odd. For he was 'not a typical Fabian' and was highly critical of them at times[7]. His early experience in Toynbee Hall took place at the height of the anti-aliens agitation, a highly racist and anti-semitic campaign. His friendship with William Temple might, one would think, have led him to consider the issue of race. For there were isolated figures among Christian social thinkers, notably J. H. Oldham, who were relating Christian theology to race as early as 1924. Reviewing Oldham's book, William Temple observed that race was the greatest of all practical problems facing humankind[8]. However, this early concern does not seem to have affected Tawney's studies, published over the same period. So *Religion and the Rise of Capitalism* (1926) does not consider the relationship between Calvinism and racial superiority, nor does *Equality* (1931) consider racial equality. However, a study of Tawney's work is relevant to our current debates at two levels: his insight into religion, socialism, equality and social change have important consequences for the anti-racist struggle, while the limitations of his approach highlight some weaknesses in our own.

Tawney's insights

First, Tawney saw that Protestant Christianity, and particularly Calvinism, had both aided the growth of capitalist society and values, and in turn had been shaped and distorted in the process. Of the growth of the capitalist spirit he wrote: 'The force which produced it was the creed associated with the name of Calvin. Capitalism was the social counterpart of Calvinist theology'[9]. In *Religion and the Rise of Capitalism* he also analysed the 'growth of individualism', the process by which Christian social action was reduced to the realm of rescue work, a process from which it is only now recovering. 'It was therefore, in the sphere of providing succour for the non-combatants and for the wounded, not in inspiring the main army, that the social work of the church was conceived to lie'. So the church 'abandoned the fundamental brainwork of criticism and construction'[10].

It is, of course, impossible to make sense of the contemporary racial scene unless we relate it to the international spread of capitalism, the colonial and, in the case of Caribbean people, the colonial and slave background to migration, and the ideology of racial superiority for which Christianity provided a theological basis. It is equally impossible to understand the inadequacy of Christian resistance to racial oppression without some grasp of the false dualism to which Tawney drew attention. Today, when some radical Christians in the Reformation traditions are speaking of the need for a second Reformation,[11] we need to learn from Tawney how grievously the tradition of the first Reformation has damaged our witness.

Secondly, Tawney held that the fundamental socialist dogma was that of the dignity of people[12] and that this involved the struggle for equality. His Christianity and his socialism were egalitarian, and it is worth noting how essential theology was to his approach, to such an extent that he held that only a believer could be consistently and faithfully egalitarian. 'In order to believe in human equality,' he wrote in 1912, 'it is necessary to believe in God'[13] 'The essence of all morality is this: to believe that every human being is of infinite importance and therefore that no consideration of expediency can justify the oppression of one by another. But to believe this it is necessary to believe in God'[14]. It was the recognition of inequality between God and people, he argued, which made any claim for inequality between persons so absurd.

Today, on the other hand, the Christian roots of the labour movement are diminishing. No longer is religion a major influence on the Labour Party[15]. The question of the survival of a commitment to equality, once the spiritual basis of that commitment has been removed, is both urgent and difficult. However, what is even more apparent is the persistence, and in recent years the resurgence, of a 'Christian' defence of inequality. I refer, of course, to the claim of Thatcherism not only to promote inequality as the condition of social progress but also to base that commitment on Christian doctrine. What we have, in the philosophy of the Conservative Party, is a passionate belief in human inequality.

Thus Sir Keith Joseph sees 'tyranny hidden in the pursuit of equality'. That pursuit is 'an instrument . . . of impoverishment and of tyranny'[16]. It was close to the fiftieth anniversary of Tawney's *Equality* when a book of the same name appeared from the pen of Sir Keith Joseph, and was commended by an East London clergyman as 'a profoundly Christian book' which 'takes the doctrine of original sin seriously'. Equality was not possible because 'men are different to an *infinite* degree'[17] (my italics). Similarly, Dr Rhodes Boyson tells us that equality restricts the human spirit while progress comes from inequality.[18] Even the dangerously 'wet' Peter Walker, whose concern for racial justice puts him streets ahead of most of his fellow Tories, prefers inequality to an egalitarian philosophy.[19] But it was George Gale who, in an exposition of the role of the rightwing journalist, summed up Conservative belief most succinctly. 'The Conservative Party,' he wrote[20] 'is not egalitarian and never can be. It is a waste of time pretending that equality is what it is about. It is about inequality.'

We should not therefore be under illusions, imagining that by some process of moistening or by the continued use of the prayer of St Francis, even in its accurate version, there might be progress towards social or racial equality in the Conservative Party. They cannot and will not promote equality because they do not believe in it. They are not hypocrites, but passionate and consistent believers in everything that St Francis and Tawney opposed. And if there were any doubts about the *belief*, the *practice* is overwhelming evidence for the commitment to inequality. The research by Townsend,[21] Atkinson,[22] Goldthorpe,[23] Field[24] and others has shown how little inequalities of wealth and income have changed over a century, and how, under the present regime, there has been a positive policy in favour of the wealthy and powerful, and against the underprivileged and the deprived. The Judaeo-Christian tradition holds that the test of belief is practical: it is those who do justice who know the Lord (Jer. 22:16). By the prophetic criteria of the pursuit of justice, the correcting of oppression, and the defence of the poor, the present regime in Britain must be seen as utterly irreligous and apostate. Tawney saw this clearly. There is, he claimed, 'no touchstone, except the treatment of childhood, which reveals the true character of a social philosophy more clearly than the spirit in which it regards the misfortunes of those who fall by the way'[25]. There could be no more damning indictment of Thatcherism than that.

Equally he saw, in 1912, the injustice in Sir Geoffrey Howe's belief that the creation of wealth was more important than its distribution,[26] a belief so accurately expressed in the recent budget. The social problem, Tawney insisted, was not about quantities but about proportions, not about the amounts of wealth but about moral justice[27].

This brings me to a third aspect of Tawney's thought: the relationship between facts and justice. The Fabian tradition was concerned to a very great extent with the collection of data. Sidney Webb believed that statistics should be gathered in order that the informed elite could run society. The underlying assumption was that if good men and women were given the 'facts', social change would follow. We should now recognise that this assumption is naive and false. Indeed in many areas of social policy, there is an inverse relationship between research and action. On matters of race and migration, Ruth Glass observed in 1964 that 'when facts contradict fiction, it is the facts which are regarded as dubious'[28]. Tawney was critical of the Fabian obsession with fact-gathering and their neglect of principle and vision. 'They tidy the room but they open no windows in the soul'[29].

Finally, let us consider Tawney's view of the role of the church. Like Temple and Gore, he held that individualism, the 'privatisation' of religion, far from being integral to the Christian tradition, was a modern aberration. From Gore he had adopted the concept of a Christian society in which the principles of the sermon on the mount were applied in social life.[30] So, in *The Acquisitive Society* (1921) he could argue for 'a new kind and a Christian kind of civilization'[31]. Hence this attachment to mediæval society with its sense of a common order and common purpose. The section in *Religion and the Rise of Capitalism* on 'The mediæval background'[32] contains a great deal of Tawney's own idea of Christian society. Like the Christendom Group, Tawney had an element of nostalgia for a Christian order of the past. In our plural society, his view must seem archaic and romantic, and he never really pursued it to its logical conclusion. Nevertheless, he did recognise and maintain the inseparable link between Christian theology and a just social order. Like Temple, he was a Christian humanist and a Christian materialist.

The rise of racism

I want now to consider some aspects of the rise of racism, drawing on the insights from Tawney. It is necessary to extend Tawney's analysis of religion and capitalism to the issues of race and colonialism. In the development of colonialism into a cohesive system, racial ideology was of central importance. Not that racism was a product of capitalist expansion. But racism was liberated by the growth of capitalism and the colonial church, as the church of the expanding, white capitalist world, was an essential part of this process. Nowhere was Tawney's analysis more relevant than in South Africa where the developing racist ideology was justified theologically by Dutch Calvinism. Its doctrine of the elect, its insistence that spirituality was as earthly and as bound to creation as dust and blood, and its belief that the black man was the descendant of the accursed Ham were vital elements in the ideology of apartheid. As Trevor Huddleston wrote in 1956, 'Calvinism, with its great insistence on "election", is the ideally suitable religious doctrine for South Africa'[33]. Thus the Christian religion, in its Dutch Calvinist form, aided the rise of institutional racism and became an integral part of its ideological apparatus[34].

However, it would be a mark of appalling insularity to see in South Africa a unique and deviant example of the Christian contribution to the rise of racism. The historic association of Christianity with whiteness has had devastating effects and led to the dehumanising and negative image of black people.[35] But let me refer briefly to two areas in which Christian churches have supported or connived at racist movements in America and Europe.

The first example is the growth, and in the last few years the revival, of the Ku Klux Klan and related movements in the United States. Studies in the late 60s showed that Protestant clergy were disproportionately represented in the membership and leadership of the Klan, while a detailed analysis of Klan membership in Knoxville, Tennessee showed that 71 per cent belonged to Baptist churches and 24 per cent to Methodist ones.

In recent years we have seen a revival of the KKK. It has been estimated that its membership doubled between 1975 and 1981, and the Anti-Defamation League now estimates its membership at around 10,000 with around 100,000 sympathisers.[36] What is much more significant is the more widespread phenomenon of the resurgence, in Britain and America, of the type of crude biblical fundamentalism, combined with an authoritarian rightwing posture, which has for more than a century provided support for racism and anti-semitism. The atmosphere created by Reagan and Thatcher, while it avoids the crudities of the fanatical racist groups, provides the ideological air in which they can breathe and breed. So in Britain we see a disturbing growth both of organised fascist groupings, including attempts to deny the Nazi holocaust and rehabilitate Hitler,[37] and of movements of religious intolerance and fanaticism of a sinister kind. Historically, Christian believers have often been in the forefront of organised racial hatred, Jewish conspiracy theories, and fanatical anti-communism with all its accompanying evils[38].

My second example is the contribution of Christianity to the growth of anti-Semitism and the inability of most Christians in Germany in the 1930s to offer any resistance to Nazism. Again, my purpose is not to throw stones but to urge us to self-scrutiny, lest we succumb to similar seductions. And Tawney's critique of religious dualism is highly relevant. The German Christians made a sharp separation between the spiritual kingdom and the affairs of state. The Jewish origin of Jesus and of the gospel was such an embarrassment to them that many denied it entirely. It was intolerable to teach that Jesus and Paul were Jewish, while belief in the incarnation was seen as inessential.[39] The Jewish spirit was to be purged from the church's life. So, on Crystal night in 1938, when the synagogues were destroyed − as indeed Luther had advised − there were no protests from Church leaders.[40] Indeed the Bishop of Thuringia's response was to reissue Luther's anti-Jewish writings.[41]

Richard Gutteridge, who has surveyed with horrifying detail the record of the German evangelical church on anti-Semitism comments: 'Throughout the conflict nobody in a position of authority made a full and plain denunciation of anti-Semitism as such.[42]

'During the whole period there is no evidence whatever of any authoritative statement being issued by the evangelical church calling for the earnest consideration of the Jewish problem from the purely biblical standpoint and in the light of the Christian gospel of mercy and love. Nor can we discover any official church warning against the mounting agitation in certain circles to treat the problem as predominantly one of race.'[43]

Karl Barth, whose theology to a great extent contributed to the weakness of the Christian resistance, claimed in 1944 that the German tragedy might have been avoided had the church not accepted the false dualism between spirituality and matters of earthly justice.[44]

I now turn to the question of racial equality in Britain. If, as Tawney held, equality is basic to Christianity and to socialism, the equality of races is an acid test of our comprehension of, and fidelity to, this belief. However, the persistence of inequality in Britain assumes grotesque proportions when we examine the question of racial disadvantage. I stress *disadvantage* because this is of far greater significance than discrimination. The 1971 census data showed that 70 per cent of black people lived in 10 per cent of enumeration districts, and these were the districts of high deprivation.[45] The evidence of racial inequality in employment, housing and other areas is considerable and indisputable.[46] All this was documented long before the riots of 1981 and was fully available before Lord Scarman's report. However, to understand the present situation of the black minority in Britain we need to go back to the end of the 50s.

This history of recent black immigration to Britain is one which reflects no credit on the Labour movement and which reinforces Tawney's view of capitalism as an immoral affront on human dignity and worth. In the postwar labour shortage, West Indian labour was recruited to help maintain London Transport and the National Health Service. 'It was their labour that was wanted, not their presence'[47]. But by the early 60s the cries for control were powerful, and in 1962 racism was nationalised by the Commonwealth Immigrants Act. The Labour Party which, under Hugh Gaitskell, had opposed the legislation, strengthened it in 1965 and have upheld it consistently ever since. By then, the old racialism was the new realism.

Nowhere was the change more obvious than in the race relations industry and its principal spokesman, Philip Mason. Mason, who had always insisted on the impartial, Fabian-style, fact-gathering role of his Institute of Race Relations, was, in January 1965, openly supporting even tighter immigration controls. 'We are determined to cut down sharply the number of fresh entries until this mouthful has been digested'[48]. In the month after the white paper on immigration, Mason was advising the National Council on Commonwealth Immigrants not to become 'a spokesman or champion for the immigrants as against the rest of the community'[49]

So there grew up in Britain, in both the Conservative and Labour Parties, the view that black people were intrinsically problematic and that their numbers must be curtailed in the interests of racial harmony. The ideology behind the demands for tighter and tighter controls was described aptly by Ruth Glass as 'a new doctrine of original sin together with a new faulty political arithmetic'[50]. By the 1971 Immigration Act the racial aspect of control had been incorporated into the legislation by the notorious 'patriality' clause. No longer did politicians claim that their concern was with 'numbers not colour' — as even Sir Cyril Osborne had insisted at the end of the 50s. Yes, the evidence for the 'number theory of prejudice' was weak. There was, and is, no correlation between the numbers of black people and the incidence of racialism. Indeed, the calls for further restriction served to generate more racial hatred and consequently further demands: after all, it was the presence of black people which caused racial hatred. The solution was therefore to reduce the numbers and so eliminate racialism.

In fact, of course, the theory is dangerous nonsense. Whereas, in 1958, Lord Justice Salmon had called the rioters in Notting Dale 'a minute and insignificant section of the population'[51], it was clear by the end of the 60s that support for explicitly racial policies was far from insignificant. There was little evidence of a consciousness of racial equality in the survey of race relations which claimed that three-fifths of British people saw themselves as superior to Africans and Asians.[52] Since then we have seen the evil influence of Powell, the rise of the National Front and its statellites, and the incorporation of the essential principles of racism into the assumption and programmes of the two major parties. In contrast to the speed and efficiency with which immigration controls have been introduced and strengthened, the weakness and half-heartedness of legislation for racial justice has been depressingly evident.

Now Tawney, and his colleague Richard Titmuss, held strongly to the view that one must legislate for equality and for social justice. Indeed, a fundamental element in the idea of a welfare state was that of redistributive justice. To restore rights to the disadvantaged, whether by race or class, was not charity. Rather, in the words of St Ambrose: 'It is not with your wealth that you give alms to the poor, but with a fraction of their own which you give back: for you are usurping for yourself something meant for the common good of all.'[53]

In the same vein Titmuss wrote: 'To me, the "welfare state" has not meaning unless it is positively and constructively concerned with redistributive justice.'[54] He used the notion of positive discrimination in favour of the poor. However, when we turn to racial inequality, injustice and disadvantage, there is little evidence that these ideas have played much part in recent years. Although the evidence of racial inequality is overwhelming, no government has used the Race Relations Act as a compaigning charter for racial justice. The Commission for Racial Equality has been a feeble, anaemic body. Had it not been for last year's riots, even the very cautious support for positive discrimination in the Scarman Report would not have seen the light of day. British policy has been based on what has been termed 'racial inexplicitness' – the view that 'race may be a predicate for positive policy as long as . . . no one takes official notice of the fact'.[55] It is right to insist that the defence of racial minorities must not neglect the wider defence of the poor of all colours: it is evasive and irresponsible to try to dissolve racial oppression into social and class oppression. Those who seek to attack racism obliquely, in the hope that it will disappear before its supporters have noticed, are unreliable allies and ineffective fighters.

Let me turn, finally, to the role of the church. With some dramatic exceptions, the British churches took up no positions on race and racism until the late 60s. There was virtually no opposition from the churches to the clearly racist immigration controls of 1962 or to the tightening of controls in 1965. However, in recent years, there has certainly been an increased willingness by the major churches in Britain to take up explicitly political positions. The Church of England, through its bishops and its general synod, has undoubtedly moved slightly but significantly to the left on questions of race, while the Catholic Commission for Racial Justice led the opposition to the Nationality Bill. The programme to combat racism of the World Council of Churches, the work of the community and race relations unit at the British Council of Churches, and the appearance of a number of voluntary campaigning bodies within the churches — CARAF, Zebra, ERRG and so on — are indications of a new determination to attack racism. The Anglican church internationally presents a more committed face than its English representative. Meeting at Limru, Kenya, in 1971, the Anglican Consultative Council not only condemned racism and called on Anglicans to examine their life and structures, but specifically commended the programme to combat racism. 'The majority of us find this action of the WCC to be the most important thing it has done in its history.' [56] This was re-asserted when the council met in Dublin in 1973. But nine years later, the programme is still not officially supported by the Church of England.

It may be said, as Gutteridge said of the treatment of Jews in Germany, 'It is hard to escape the conclusion that to the great majority of church people, this was a matter of no real concern.' [57] The churches in Britain are not in the forefront of the movement for racial justice, however much some church organisations have been playing vital roles. In country and suburb and small market town, the anti-racist struggle is not on the agenda. The comprehension gap between the church in the inner city and the more prosperous suburban church is growing wider as the response to last year's riots indicated.

What then should the future hold for Christians in an era of rising racism? And how does Tawney's thinking throw light on our responsibility? I believe a prime necessity is for a theologically-based, carefully designed, disentanglement of the church from the capitalist system. Tawney was very clear about the incompatibility of Christian principles with the capitalist spirit: 'Compromise is as impossible between the church of Christ and the idolatry of wealth, which is the practical religion of capitalist societies, as it was between the church and the state idolatry of the Roman empire.' [58]

The reality is very different, and simply wishing it were not so will not effect change. Many Christians believe that there is a 'third way', a neutral position between capitalism and socialism, from which Christians can work. If by this is meant the impossibility of a simple identification of the Kingdom of God with a specific political system, one would agree. But for a church which is deeply involved in the structures of capitalism to postulate a third way, is to assume a situation which in fact has to be created. If racial oppression, internationally and internally, is bound up with the system of investments, profits, labour needs, and so on, there can be no real attack on racism without a corresponding attack on the structures of capitalism. Simply to seek racial harmony at the local level, or to place the odd black bishop on the bench, in themselves will not be adequate. *Pace* Lord Scarman, institutional racism does exist in Britain, and it cannot be eliminated without a struggle. But as in the attack on all structural sin, the forces of injustice are very powerful. Christians who enter the anti-racist struggle must expect the most violent and vicious opposition, and they will need all the theological and spiritual resources they can get.

Secondly, I think that there needs to be a re-assertion by the church — or, at least, by those members of the church who believe it! — that equality is of the nature of God and of humankind. To assert this is not only to contradict the fundamental dogma of the present government, and therefore place the church firmly on the other side, but it is also to contradict many of the assumptions and trends within authoritarian socialism. Most of all, it is to recognise that the ideology of inequality is most deeply entrenched within the structures of the church itself. No part of English society is more unequal, more allied to privilege, more culture-bound, more rooted in the private eduational system, or more alien to working-class people than the Church of England. It is unreasonable and absurd to expect a sustained anti-racist campaign from such a body unless those within the church are prepared to combat the social inequality which is so much a part of its history and life. But this is not to say that we must put the anti-racist movement into cold storage until we have created a classless society within the church: the process of radicalisation is indivisible. The racial crisis may well be the sieve through which a range of impurities in British Christianity will be purged.

Racism in the church, in its theology, its culture, its institutions and its member- ship, goes deep, and consciousness of its presence remains dim. The attack on church racism must be many-pronged, and it has hardly begun. The roots of racism in white society must be penetrated and examined: and this ministry of exorcism, this intensifying of white awareness which Judy Katz and her followers have rightly seen to be essential to anti-racist training, will not go unresisted. [59] There needs to be a thorough and careful scrutiny of the spiritual formation of clergy and ministers for a multi-racial society: recent research shows that they are ill-prepared and ill-equipped for their new role.[60] The criterion for choice of bishops in the Church of England remain consistently mysterious, but it seems unlikely that they include evangelical witness against racism. But is it reasonable to have to wait for cases of formal heresy before a bishop's credibility is questioned? 'What did you do in the Great War, Daddy?' would seem to be a reasonable question for the faithful to ask of its father in God. But all too often, the answer would be: what war? The war against racism has not entered the consciousness of most church people in Britain. In 1978 the general synod of the Church of England passed a resolution urging the dioceses to raise £100,000 a year for the race relations projects fund of the British Council of Churches. In 1982, the response from a number of dioceses remains at nil. And this is not on the whole as a result of opposition so much as a sheer unawareness of what all the fuss is about.

In a hostile and unfair review of 'the socialism of R. H. Tawney'[61] Alasdair MacIntyre claimed that Tawney never came to terms with the developed nature of capitalism in the era of big corporations and multinationals, and that the moral denunciation of a system is no substitue for efficient attack upon it. Testifying to Tawney's essential goodness, MacIntyre asked his readers if they preferred to have their shoes mended by a good cobbler or a good man. Christians will be unhappy at the simple separation of moral goodness from political action, but MacIntyre's essential point is that we need to move beyond moral protest to the political attack on structures. And this is particularly true of the struggle against racism.

As the central committee of the World Council of Churches stated, in 1969:[62] 'It is no longer sufficient to deal with the race problem at the level of person to person relationships. It is *institutional racism* as reflected in the economic and political power structures which must be challenged. Combating racism must entail a *redistribution* of social, economic, political and cultural *power* from the powerful to the powerless.'

The church's campaign against racism must shift from sentiment to the confrontation of power, including its own power. And it is at this point that faces begin to drop, sympathisers edge uneasily away, and tolerance changes to implacable opposition. It is at this point that our false friends betray the cause and our true friends are revealed. It is at this point that we may usefully recall Tawney's insistence on 'recourse to principles'. For the church is not called to compromise with organised injustice, still less to enter into dialogue with it, but to seek to end it.

This lecture was given in March, 1982.

References

1 A. Sivanandan, *Race, class and the state: the black experience in Britain* (Institute of Race Relations 1976) p 367. This and other papers are now published in his recent volume, *A Different Hunger* (Pluto Press 1982).

2 *The Protestant Ethic and the Spirit of Capitalism* (1920), E. T. Talcott Parsons, Unwin University Books, 1976 edn.

3 *Religion and the Rise of Capitalism* (1926), cited hereafter as RRC. References are to the Penguin 1969 edn.

4 R. H. Preston, *Religion and the Persistence of Capitalism* (SCM Press 1979).

5 *Land and Labour in China* (Allen and Unwin 1932); *The Condition of China* (Early Grey Memorial Lecture, Newcastle, 1933).

6 Partha Sarathi Gupta. *Imperialism and the British Labour Movement 1914–1964* (Macmillan 1975) p 337.
Those who are in any doubt as to how racialist some of the early Fabians were should read the accounts of China in Beatrice Webb's diaries. The Webbs were crudely racialist in their accounts of the Chinese people, and used language which makes the National Front seem quite restrained. The moral defects of the Chinese as a race, demonstrated particularly in their homosexuality, made them incapable of orderly government. Beatrice Webb wrote in her unpublished diaries: 'It is this rottenness of physical and moral character that makes one despair of China — their constitution seems devastated by drugs and abnormal sexual indulgence. They are essentially an unclean race.' (Diaries, Vol 30, 6 November 1911, cited in J. M. Winter, *Socialism and the Challenge of War*, Routledge and Kegan Paul, 1974, p 43) They had 'horrid expressions' on their faces, and were 'a horrid race'. Sidney Webb too saw the Chinese as a 'striking example of arrested development', and based his conclusion on what appears to be a crude early form of sociobiology.

7 Ross Terrill, *R. H. Tawney and his times: socialism as fellowship* (Harvard University Press 1973) p 276.

8 *International Review of Mission* 31:51 (July 1924), reviewing J. H. Oldham, *Christianity and the Race Problem* (SCM Press 1924).

9 Foreword to Max Weber, op cit p 2.

10 RRC pp 195-6.

11 See Jeremy Rifkin and Ted Howard, *The Emerging Order: God in an Age of Scarcity* (New York, G. P. Putnams Sons, 1979); and their article 'Hope for a second Reformation' in *Sojourners*, September 1979, p 11: 'Together protestantism and capitalism transformed the planet. Now a new order is emerging as the world moves from the age of growth to the age of scarcity. As a consequence the end of the prevailing economic epoch presages the end of the prevailing theological epoch as well.'

12 *Equality* (Allen and Unwin 1964 edn.) p 197.

13 *R. H. Tawney's Commonplace Book* (ed J. M. Winter and D. M. Joslin, Economic History Review Supplement 5, Cambridge University Press, 1972) p 53.

14 ibid p 67.

15 See John Hall and Joan Higgins, 'What influences today's Labour MPs?', *New Society*, 2 December 1976, pp 457–9; and George Moyser, 'Voting on moral issues in the House of Commons', *Papers in Religion and Politics* No 10, Spring Term 1980, faculty of theology and dept of government, University of Manchester.

16 *The Times*, 9 June 1978.

17 Prebendary John Pearce in *Third Way* June 1980 pp 31–2, reviewing Keith Joseph and Jonathan Sumpton, *Equality* (John Murray 1979).

18 *The Times*, 17 December 1975.

19 *The Ascent of Britain* (Sidgewick and Jackson, 1977) pp 20–22.

20 'The popular communication of the Conservative message' in *Conservative Essays* (ed Maurice Cowling, Cassell 1978) p 190.

21 Peter Townsend, *Poverty in The United Kingdom* (Penguin, 1979).

22 A. B. Atkinson, *Poverty in Britain and the Reform of Social Security* (Cambridge University Press 1969); *Unequal Shares: wealth in Britain* (Penguin 1972); and *Social Justice and Public Policy* (Harvester, 1982).

23 John H. Goldthorpe, *Social Mobility and Class Structure in Modern Britain* (Oxford University Press 1980).

24 Frank Field (ed) *The Wealth Report* (Routledge and Kegan Paul 1979); *One in Eight: a Report on Britain's Poor* (Low Pay Unit, 1979).

25 RRC p 265.

26 *The Guardian*, 3 July 1978.

27 *Commonplace Book*, p 18.

28 Ruth Glass and John Westergaard, *London's Housing Needs* (Centre for Urban Studies, University College, London, 1965) p xi.

29 *Commonplace Book* p 51.

30 See Charles Gore, *The Sermon on the Mount* (1896) and *The Social Doctrine of the Sermon on the Mount* (1904).

31 *The Acquisitive Society* (1921) p 239.

32 pp 17–74.

33 *Naught for Your Comfort* (Fontana 1971 edn) p 50.

34 For the application of Tawney's thesis to the South African scene see A. Sivanandan, 'Race, class and caste in South Africa – an open letter to No Sizwe', *Race and Class* 22:3 (Winter 1981) pp 293–300; and Ken Jordaan, 'Iberian and Anglo-Saxon racism: a study of Portuguese Angola and South Africa', ibid 20:4 (Spring 1979) pp 391–412.

35 See the writings of Frantz Fanon especially *Black Skin, White Masks* (MacGibbon and Kee 1968).

36 See S. M. Lipset and Earl Raab, *The Politics of Unreason: Right-Wing Extremism in America 1790–1970* (Neinmann 1971) pp 117–123; Kennett T. Jackson, *The Ku Klux Klan in the City 1915–1930* (New York, Oxford University Press 1967) p 63. For more up-to-date information on the recent resurgence of the KKK contact Klanwatch, PO Box 548, Montgomery, Alabama 36101.

37 The notorious pamhlet *Did six milion really die?* by 'Richard Harwood' is the most extreme attempt to deny the holocaust. On the work of the revisionist historians see Ian Barnes, 'Revisionism and the Right', *Contemporary Affairs Briefing* 1:2 (January 1982). On contemporary fascist groups in general, a good introduction is Paul Wilkinson, *The New Fascists* (Grant MacIntyre 1981) and the monthly journal *Searchlight*.

38 See Charles Y. Glock and Rodney Stark, *Christian Beliefs and Anti-Semitism* (Harper and Row, 1966). For further references see the essay 'Is there a new religious fascism?' in my book *The Social God* (Sheldon Press 1981 pp 97–115).

39 A. S. Duncan-Jones, *The Struggle for Religious Freedom in Germany* (Gollanz 1938) pp 299ff.

40 William Shirer, *The Rise and Fall of the Third Reich* (Secker and Warburg 1960) p 435.

41 Richard Gutteridge, *Open thy mouth for the dumb: the German Evangelical Church and the Jews 1879–1950* (Blackwell 1976) p 191.

42 ibid p 268.

43 ibid p 41.

44 cited ibid p 282.

45 Sally Holtermann, 'Areas of urban deprivation in Great Britain: an analysis of the 1971 Census', *Social Trends* 6 (1975).

46 For a summary of much of the recent research see John Downing, *Now you do know* (War on want 1980).

47 A. Sivanandan, 'From resistance to rebellion: Asian and Afro-Caribbean struggles in Britain', *Race and Class* 23:3 (1981–2) p 112.

48 *The Guardian*, 23 January 1965. For the history of the IRR and the changes in its thought and positions see A. Sivanandan, *Race and Resistance: the IRR story* (Race Today 1974). Mason's Fabian view comes out in his claim that the survey of race relations would produce a 'vast mass of information and set the whole in a new and illuminating perspective', and thus 'avoid mistakes'. See his foreword to E. J. B. Rose, *Colour and Citizenship* (Oxford University Press 1968).

49 Address to the NCCI, 2 September 1965.

50 *The Times*, 5 August 1967. For a detailed account of the new secular *'theology of racism'* see Martin Barker, *The New Racism* (Junction Books 1981). In a review of the work of the sociobiologist E. O. Wilson, *On Human Nature* (Harvard 1978) the Chicago theologian James M. Gustafson described it as 'the secular equivalent of a systematic theology'. See his 'Sociobiology: a secular theology', *Hastings Center Report*, February 1979.

51 *The Times*, Law Report, 16 September 1958.

52 Nicholas Deakin, *Colour, Citizenship and British Society* (1970) p 325.

53 Migne, *Patrologia Latina* 14:747.

54 R. M. Titmuss, 'Goals of today's welfare state' in *Towards Socialism* (ed Perry Anderson and Robin Blackburn, Fontana 1964) p 354. See also his *Commitment to Welfare* (Allen and Unwin 1968) pp 113–4.

55 David L. Kirp, *Doing good by doing little: race and schooling in Britain* (University of California Press 1981) p 2.

56 *The Time is Now* (SPCK 1971) p 18.

57 Gutteridge, op cit p 96.

58 RRC p 280.

59 Judy Katz, *White awareness: a handbook for anti-racist training* (University of Oklahoma Press 1978).

60 See the recent study *Blind leaders for the blind?* (Birmingham, AFFOR 1982).

61 Reprinted in Alasdair MacIntyre, *Against the self-images of the age* (Duckworth 1971) pp 38–42.

62 Statement of the WCC central committee, Canterbury, August 1969.

Irene Brennan
The gospel and Marxism

One of the major factors inhibiting the development of socialism in this country, a truly humanist and democratic socialism, rooted in the experience of the people, reflecting the best apsects of our culture and flexible enough both in its theory and practice to respond to the particular problems and possibilities of British society, is the failure to unite political analysis with socialist vision, political activism with spiritual insight; the head with the heart. R. H. Tawney's great strength lay in his refusal to accept this disintegrating and irrational alienation, so typical of capitalism, and his constant effort to synthesise his socialist commitment and his religious faith within the framework of a rigorous scholarship.

Throughout his work he tried to combat the 'divorce between religion and social ethics'[1] and 'the dualism which regards the secular and religious aspects of life, not as successive stages within a larger society, but as parallel and independent provinces, governed by different laws; judged by different standards and amenable to different authorities.'[2] He exhibits in his writing a careful attention to material realities and a constant endeavour to analyse and understand the social structures and relations that they reveal. He recognised the utopian illusions of those early socialists who tried to fight the onset of capitalism; while sympathising with their fundamental objectives he, like Engels, knew that without tools of political analysis and social organisation, impossible to develop at that time, they were doomed.

'Commonsense and a respect for realities are not less graces of the spirit than moral zeal. The paroxyms of virtuous fury with which the children of light denounced each new victory of economic enterprise as yet another strategem of mammon, disabled them for the staff work of their campaign, which needs a cool head as well as a stout heart. Their obstinate refusal to revise old formulae in the light of new facts exposed them helpless to counter attack, in which the whole fabric of their philosophy, truth and fantasy alike, was overwhelmed together. They despised knowledge and knowledge destroyed them.'[3] This is the utopian consciousness described by Engels as that 'which certainly criticised the existing capitalist mode of production and its consequences. But it could not explain them, and therefore could not get mastery of them.'

There are traces, certainly, of this attitude among some socialists today but it is no longer, I believe, so important. Other socialists may have been destroyed by their lack of knowledge of socio-economic realities; the left in Britain may be in danger of being destroyed because of its lack of respect for ethical and spiritual realities. As Tawney reminds us, 'Agreement as to ends implies the acceptance of a standard of values by which the position to be assigned to different objects may be determined . . . each standard must take account of economic possibilities but it cannot of itself be merely economic, since the comparative importance of economic and of other interests — the sacrifice, for example, of material goods worth incurring, in order to extend leisure, or to develop education, or to humanise toil, is precisely the point on which it is needed to throw light. It must be based upon some conception of human nature as a whole.'[4]

The socialist, and that includes the Marxist, needs a stout heart stirred by visionary hope and animated by socialist ideals, otherwise analysis becomes nothing more than the pursuit of empty formulae and political work degenerates into mechanical manoeuvrings. 'Where there is no vision the people perish' (Prov. 29:18). That is because perseverance fails, courage degenerates into the foolhardly brawlings of factional in-fighting and unity is lost. We need to return to the wellspring of hope and commitment that vivified the men and women who built the labour movement in this country; we need to recapture and reinterpret for our generation their vision of a liberated and truly human society.

Throughout the centuries, those who have been committed to the struggle for a better society in this country have been animated directly, or indirectly, by the Christian gospel. Very often that debt was acknowledged, as one can discover by reading the works of those who were able to write, or whose speeches were reported. They looked forward to the *'New Jerusalem'* and the establishment of it *on earth*; they prayed for this in the words of the *Our Father*: Thy will be done on earth. They were prepared to suffer and die for its accomplishment. As Winstanley put it 'True freedom lies in the community in spirit and community in the earthly treasury, and this is Christ the true manchild spread abroad in the creation, restoring all things unto himself.'[5] And, 'they that are resolved to work and eat together, making the earth a common treasury, doth join hands with Christ to lift the creation from bondage.'[6] These socialist and communists understood the true meaning of the second beatitude: 'Happy the lowly; they shall inherit the earth' (Matt. 5:4) and instinctively felt that history belonged to them, that human liberation would be achieved.

As Tawney showed in his classic work *Religion and the Rise of Capitalism*,[7] the socio-economic relations of capitalism produced a distorted Christianity that in turn gave support to the established order. The profoundly alienating effects of capitalism were shown in a religious creed which accepted a sharp dichotomy between social and economic affairs and personal morality, and between secular pursuits and religious practices. So we find Christianity presented as an intense and inward looking other-worldliness which turned away from secular matters and saw salvation as a personal, individual question. This distorted Christianity was found in all major denominations and reflected, as Marx rightly argued, the class attitudes of the establishment.[8] The gospel began to cease to have relevance for ethics and to be interpreted as an expression of moral transcendence or personal mysticism. One theologian in this tradition could write that, 'a moment's reflection will convince us that the beatitudes say nothing about ethics.'[9] As Moltmann has pointed out, this religion, 'which leaves earthly conditions or corporeal existence to the mercy of their own contradictoriness and restricts itself to the church, to the cultus or to believing inwardness, is, therefore, a denial of the cross.'[10] It can hardly be thought to *be* Christian; it is precisely on this earth, in its social and political realities, that the cross is found.

Marx and Engels were educated within this particular religious tradition and when they rejected it, and justifiably so, they took the road of an atheistic rationalism and humanism. Given the social background of both Marx and Engels, it would be a mistake to expect them to have been acquainted, in the crucial time of decision, with the deep commitment to the actual teachings of the gospel which did exist in the workers' movements of the time. Only later, when they became communists, did Marx and Engels begin to have to come to terms with this. It is reflected by a kind of ironic and affectionate recognition of this 'utopian Christianity' which, while consciously rejected, constantly makes its presence felt in their writings. Their atheism was a rejection of a *false* God, the God of power, oppression and exploitation: the God of this world. They rejected the false Christ who is sacrificed to this God and who preaches subservience to it. They rejected the spirit of personal profit seeking: the spirit of this world. In this rejection of idolatry and the false religion that is its cult they were following in the tradition of the Hebrew prophets and of Jesus Christ himself. But as far as we know, Marx preserved his position of atheist rationalism which showed the union of a 'theoretic atheism with a believing heart.'[11] Neither he nor Engels, 'negated the negation' and proceeded from the rejection of a false view of God and humanity to a deeper faith and commitment not only to other human beings, but to God also. They gave faithful witness to a prophetic truth which shone like a great light on the hypocrisy that surrounded them. Their penetrating analysis of the social role of religious institutions has helped to purify the faith and commitment of countless believers, and the impassioned struggle for socialist principles and values shows a living witness to the truths of the gospel.

A century after Marx's death, a third of the world's population has Marxist governments and millions more people claim to be Marxists. Understandably there are many ways of interpreting and applying Marxist theory to a whole range of varying conditions. Different communist parties have evolved their own strategies for achieving or maintaining socialism. These strategies have to be understood in the light of differing socio-economic systems and the particular traditions and values of the working class movement, as well as other cultural and political institutions and trends. Marx himself worked in a given historical situation and his views have to be assessed in the light of that; this does not invalidate his theory but recognises that Marx's own formulations can be improved and clarified. The founders of Marxism *began* the systematic analysis of social relations. To do this they used the conceptual framework called 'historical materialism' to delineate the area of investigation and to enable the appropriate methodologies to be developed for examining a new area of study — political economy. They analysed not only capitalist relations but also conditions which would be necessary for the transition from capitalism to socialism. Marx and Engels, especially Marx, had the *first* word on these questions but, as he would be the first to acknowledge, he did not have the last or only word. Because Marxism is creative, others following after have extended, modified and clarified Marxist analysis.

Whenever a static approach to Marxist theory is found, there, as Castro put it, Marxism becomes 'a pseudo-revolutionary church' and 'fails to interpret today's realities objectively.'[12] Whenever Marxism is used as a substitute for religious belief then we find it showing all the worst manifestations of distorted religion:

dogmatism, authoritarianism and ferocious attacks on 'heretics'. This is not to say that all Marxist atheists exhibit these characteristics − far from it; but the tendency is clearly present among Marxists. Marxist method should be based upon a due respect for the material realities that are the proper subject of its analysis and that means utilising the appropriate conceptual tools with an acknowledgment also of the limitations of these same tools. Too often the 'materialism' of Marxism which should be founded on the scrupulous regard for the nature of the material degenerates into a 'metaphysical materialism' to use Engel's phrase, 'which queens it over the rest of the sciences.' [13] We need not a 'metaphysical materialism' but a sophisticated methodology which understands its own limitations and the relation of Marxist analysis to other intellectual disciplines. Otherwise the 'materialism' of Marxist analysis may degenerate into a crude metaphysics shot through with a dogmatic atheism, which stands as an obstacle to a deeper understanding of social relations and serves as a brake on the development and building of socialist society.

Marxists have to decide whether atheistic prejudice is more important to them than the achievement of revolutionary change, for as well as acting as a serious impediment to the development of Marxist theory and to the building of a united movement, it reinforces some of the least democratic manifestations of socialist practice, namely the exclusion of religious believers from full participation in political life in certain socialist countries. Some of the problems of Poland can be traced back to this. Just as religious believers have no right to claim a monopoly of political power within a society, neither do the atheists; just as religious believers should defend the rights and liberties of atheists and agnostics, so non-believers should respect the rights and liberties of believers.

However, even if Marxist analysis is free from prejudice and is careful, exact and veracious, it alone cannot bring about revolutionary change. That is brought about by the action of the people: analysis needs to be placed at their disposal. The revolutionary movement in any given society will be rooted in the local culture and will have within it a number of currents of thought and belief, some of which will not be wholly compatible one with another but all of which have a positive and specific contribution to make to its unique character. Those who wish to deny the importance that Christian commitment has played in the building of the British labour movement are flying in the face of truth and denying the history of their own working people. A similarly narrow minded approach is found among those who will not acknowledge the increasingly important part that Marxists play in the struggle for socialism, or who deny the specific contribution of humanists and rationalists, or who will not recognise the growing importance of the women's movement or the peace movement. And I suppose we have all met those who seem to think that socialism can be achieved without the involvement of the trade unions!

The democratic, open, pluralist character of the movement for change in Britain will help us to achieve a democratic, open, pluralist form of socialism. This fact is specifically recognised and welcomed in the Communist Party of Great Britain's programme: *The British Road to Socialism*, and its strategy is based on the acceptance of the need to strengthen and extend this *broad democratic alliance*. Any attempt to exclude certain elements, or to narrow the spectrum of belief and attitude, or to deny the importance of the strength of ideas or of religious faith, which have led thousands of people to spend their whole lives striving to bring about socialism in this country, would be gravely weakening and undermine the values which have led people to socialist ideas and political commitment. It is a fact that, taken as a whole, Christian faith has been the heart and soul of the labour movement. It is not true for individuals, or for some groups or parties but, taken overall, it has been the source of commitment, hope, solidarity and self sacrifice for millions in this country who have been and are commited to socialism.

Throughout the world there are now very many who call themselves Christian Marxists; some in Britain, thousands more in western Europe, Africa and Asia, and hundreds of thousands, if not millions, in Latin America. Christians are now found in the leadership of some of the west European Communist parties and in the Marxist governments of Nicaragua and Zimbabwe, as well as in the Marxist leaderships of the movements all over Latin America and Asia. I claim to be a Christian Marxist. Both 'orthodox' Marxists and traditional Christians will insist that this is not possible, but life itself shows that it is. We are told that we are living a contradiction and, in a certain sense, that is true. But as Marxists we know that contradictions, in the Marxist sense of the term, should not be avoided and denied, but should be lived, in all their pain and conflict, and resolved. We are striving to overcome the antagonism that has been created between Marxism and religious faith. We are striving to unite Christian faith and political commitment, and to utilise the insights of Marxist analysis in the service of justice and community. This resolution will take different forms in different cultures and will, of itself, raise new perspectives and problems.

There is an established school of thought among Marxists which would argue that all Marxists should have the same *weltanschauung*, the same world view, but there can be no such thing as an abstract *weltanschauung* which is injected into or imposed upon a local movement. Wherever Marxists have seen Marxism as this abstract system, complete with a self-sufficient ideology expressing the values and attitudes of nineteenth century socialist rationalism, they have locked themselves in an ahistorical position. This is in flat contradiction to the spirit of Marx's methodology and they have cut themselves off from the living culture of their own people. Fortunately this tendency, though endemic among Marxists, has been countered by the desire, which remains true to the spirit and method of Marx's thought, to analyse the actual social, economic, political and cultural relations in each society and to develop appropriate political strategies in the light of that. This means that there is now established the principle that each country must follow its own path to socialism and that there exists no 'model' or 'international centre' to determine what is appropriate in each case. Condemnation of 'revisionism' is now being replaced in the world communist movement by the acknowledgement of the need for flexibility and the eradication of sectarian attitudes. This has been interpreted by some parties in western Europe, including the British, by a commitment to democratic pluralism.

Marxist-Christian dialogue is now at a new stage. There are still those who wish to see it, as it was seen in the sixties, as a dialogue between two groups of people who respect one another's integrity but, at the same time, are intent on preserving their own positions and principles. When atheism is thought to be integral to Marxism, clearly it is unprincipled of any Marxist holding this position, or any Christian who sees Marxism in that way, to try and make compromises about belief.

But now many Marxists do *not* see atheism as integral to Marxist methodology but simply as an expression of certain attitudes which influenced Marx and Engels and which were found among nineteenth century radical intellectuals on the continent of Europe. This is not to denigrate those who hold atheist views. But such views are merely *beliefs* about the nature of reality and not *methodological principles*. I daresay Marx and Engels had a number of views about personal relations, art, music, food, travel and so on, but these views, whether fundamental or trivial, are not necessarily part of a system of analysis valid for us today.

It is significant that Christian Marxism is found most often in the third world where the ancient battles of nineteenth century Europe between radicals and the church authorities were unknown. In Latin America, the Philippines and parts of Africa and Asia, the radicals are in the churches and doing battle with reactionary political authorities. The theology of liberation and not of subservience is preached and the people have begun to live their own synthesis of the gospel and Marxism, in spite of the hostility of governments and certain church hierarchies.

Christian Marxists have gone their own way and decided to stop rejecting one set of truths for another. They have decided to abandon those careful 'principles', those 'orthodoxies' created by the needs, limitation and, at times, the fears, of others, and to pursue justice and truth as they see it. They have their own limitations of course, but at least they are part of our own lived truth. They are not the result of restrictions placed upon us by others who do not experience the same driving, inner demand to stand in solidarity with the oppressed, to witness the truth of the gospel, and to use use every tool of analysis, and that means Marxism, to understand social conditions and bring about change. In Britain, to be a Marxist is to be part of a still smallish minority – though growing – and to be a Christian Marxist is thought to be eccentric or, even, bizarre. But in other parts of the world, especially the third world, that is no longer the case, and we see people in those countries living by a hope, a vision, a commitment that is Christian, socialist and Marxist. With the development of a theology that understands more clearly than before how it is possible for a false God to be worshipped as the Christian God, Marx's atheism is understood in a sympathetic way. As Miranda, the liberation theologian, has put it: 'God will only be in a world of justice, and if Marx does not find him in the western World, it is because he is, indeed, not there, nor can he be.' [14]

The founders of Marxism, together with some later Marxist writers, always recognised that they inherited a tradition of commitment to socialist ideals. This has existed for centuries in Europe and can be traced back to the apostolic community of the early Christians, which practised a form of communism. This is presented in Acts as the community's witness to the coming of the New Age, to the resurrection of the Lord Jesus, and is an expression of the courage that they were given through the gift of the Spirit. 'The whole group of believers was united in heart and soul; no-one claimed anything that he had, as everything that they owned was held in common. The apostles continued to testify to the resurrection of the Lord Jesus with great power and they were all given great respect. None of their members was ever in need as all those who owned land and houses would sell them, and bring the money from them, to present it to the apostles; it was distributed to any members who might be in need.' (Acts 4:32–35) The community lived in the mystery of the Eucharist and made its truth clear to others. Their witness has remained what it was then, not just a call to enter a separate community but a challenge to the whole of society to reform itself. The resources of the community were given 'according to what each needed' (Acts 2:45) a phrase used later by Marx in the *Critique of the Gotha Programme*, 'from each according to his ability, to each according to his needs.' [15] Throughout the centuries, Christians have tried to find ways of giving a similar witness. Some have entered religious communities and practised the common life, but this was usually not seen as representing a model for the rest of the society. Others worked in radical and socialist movements, utopian and visionary, so that we are not able to see how their ideals might be translated into practice. But they kept those ideals living for us and we 'have come into the rewards of their labour' (John 4:38).

Now we are just at the beginning of the period of experiment and effort when whole societies begin to take that path. It will take us centuries, probably, to establish full democratic socialist societies throughout the world — namely, to achieve communism — but now many can see how that might be achieved. The contribution of Marxism to that is enormous. But it was Aquinas, centuries earlier, who had said, 'in that which concerns exterior things man should not possess them exclusively for himself alone, but to have them in common with others so that each puts what he has at the disposal of others.' [16] Taken together with Aquinas's condemnation of usury and his appreciation of the importance of labour in the creation of wealth, as well as his opposition to forms of exploitation, it is no wonder that Tawney wryly comments that 'the true descendant of the doctrines of Aquinas is the labour theory of value. The last of the schoolmen was Karl Marx.' [17]

Whether or not one wishes to ascribe it to the influence of Marx, Aquinas or the gospel itself, the encyclical on human work *Laborem Excercens*, by Pope John Paul II, argues that the 'right of private property is subordinated to the right of common use, to the fact that goods are meant for everyone.' [18] It calls for 'the joint ownership of the means of work', [19] and goes on to argue that, 'merely converting the means of production into state property in a collectivist system is by no means equivalent to "socialising" that property.' [20] If this is an implicit criticism of the practice in certain of the socialist countries, it is based on the argument that they are not yet sufficiently socialist, and not on condemnation of socialism as such. Capitalism is unambiguously condemned, in terms very similar to those used by Marx, as, 'the error of economism', [21] and the treating of man as, 'the instrument of the means of production', as a, 'reversal of order', [22] because, 'labour must take priority over capital'. [23] The 'justified response of the workers' movements', was against, 'the degradation of man as the subject of work and against the unheard-of exploitation in the field of wages, working conditions and social security.' [24] Tawney puts it more succinctly: 'Compromise is impossible between the church of Christ and the idolatry of wealth which is the practical religion of capitalist societies, as it was between the church and the state idolatry of the Roman empire.' [25]

The parable of Dives and Lazarus shows that the early Christian community recognised the existence of class division, that 'great chasm' as Luke calls it (Luke 18:26), and deplored it. The epistle of James as well as that marvellous song of liberation, the *Magnificat*, remind us that the early Christians believed that this state of things would be reversed by a revolutionary upheaval. The *Magnificat* anticipates it: 'He has pulled down princes from their thrones and exalted the lowly. The hungry he has filled with good things, the rich sent empty away.' (Luke 1:52) This revolution will bring about, 'new heavens and a new earth,' (2 Pet. 3:13) for, as McArthur comments, 'Jesus did not call men to a higher way within the world; but to a way that would ovethrow the world.' [26] To 'recognise that the protests of the poor are the voice of God' [27] and that they ask from us solidarity is, necessarily, to engage in 'class struggle' and, as Metz points out, it is still true that 'apocalyptic shock' is produced inside the church by those who are prepared to do this.

Marxism is often denounced as an evil philosophy that encourages hatred and violence, but this is a complete distortion. Both Marx and Engels were opposed to a reliance on insurrection as a way to bring about change. They took issue with the anarchists and blanquists who advocated such methods and argued instead that revolution – as opposed to *coup d'état* – was only possbile when the working class movement was prepared to use its socio-economic strength to transform the situation. 'The irony of world history turns everything upside down,' Engels wrote. [29] 'We the "revolutionists" the "over throwers", we are thriving far bettter on legal methods than illegal methods. The parties of order, as they call themselves, are perishing under legal conditions created by themselves. They cry despairingly with Odilon Barrot: la legalité nous tue – legality is the death of us. Whereas under this legality, we get firm muscles and rosy cheeks.'

As for the class hatred, every socialist and Marxist is committed to the eradication of what causes hatred and division – namely class division, exploitation and oppression. What else is that but love, genuine solidarity and commitment to human community expressed in practical politics? We love the oppressed by solidarity, by standing together with others and sharing their sufferings, their aspirations and their struggles for a better human life, we love the oppressors by opposing them and calling on them to abandon oppression, which is death, and to choose the real life of commitment to others. As Christians, however, we should go further than this. The Lord Jesus calls on us: 'love your enemies' (Matt. 5:44). We are not asked to pretend that we do not have any, but to love them through opposition, through the search for truth and justice, through the prayer for mutual forgiveness that recognises our mutual sinfulness. Christians should be giving living witness to the power of forgiving and truthful love. Instead, we often offer careful ambiguities and moral exhortations, and then wonder why others reject us as hypocrites. We find Jesus Christ where the cross is, and the cross is in the suffering of the struggle for justice, in the expression of solidarity, in mutual forgiveness.

Christianity is not a set of rules, which Christians keep and the rest of the world ignores. Rather, it is a way, and on that way one recognises fellow pilgrims and companions, whatever name they give themselves. I believe that the gospel calls us 'into the way of peace' (Luke 1:79) and towards pacifism. Each one of us must decide what that means for us personally. Clearly most Christian churches do not see a commitment to non-violence as incumbent upon their members. But we are called *towards* that. Unfortunately there are those who are prepared to condemn oppressed people when, in desperation, they finally take to arms, but who do not condemn the systematic violence of oppression and injustice that produced the violence. Nor are their voices heard raised against the evils of the nuclear arms race, the acceptance of 'first strike' strategies and a massive expenditure on arms which means that the world's resources are squandered while millions of people die of hunger and disease.

If we are concerned, as Christians, to build peace, then we must try to bring an end to the arms race and the cold war, and try to create relations of friendship and trust with the peoples of the socialist countries, while transferring resources away from armaments to development in the third world. We need to oppose the activities of British based multinationals where they exploit third world workers. We have no right to preach the way of Jesus to others when we do not share their sufferings, their struggles and their hope — and our society is committed to massive violence. If we do, then we are like the hypocrites described in the gospel, who, 'do not practise what they preach. They tie up heavy burdens and place them on men's shoulders, but will they lift a finger to help? Not they!' (Matt. 23:4) But where the gospel is understood and *lived* then its truth becomes apparent. As Machovec said in his admirable book entitled *A Marxist looks at Jesus*, 'thus Marxists too begin to wonder whether the pacifism characteristic not only of the sermon on the mount but also of Jesus's entire ministry could not be joined perfectly harmoniously to the most rigorous form of Marxist commitment to progress.' [30]

During the course of the Marxist and Christian dialogue of the sixties it became clear that both Marxists and Christians share a hope in the future and belief that, as Moltmann put it: 'This is the age of *diaspora*, in sowing hope, of self-surrender and of self-sacrifice, for it is an age which stands within the *horizon of a new future.*' [31] This new age will not be achieved without a profound transformation of social, economic and cultural relations and structures. It demands socialism. But although, as Ragaz has said, 'within the Kingdom of God the whole of socialism is contained,' [32] yet one cannot simply conflate the two. The achievement of socialism and then, eventually, its higher form communism, is only a stage in the journey towards full human liberation. What that might be we have hardly begun to understand: 'the things that no eye has seen, no ear has heard, things beyond the mind of people, all that God has prepared for those who love him.' (1 Cor. 2:9) We are called to cooperate with God in the work of human liberation and redemption, the establishment of the Kingdom of God *on earth*, but we know that this is given to us as *a gift, a grace*. For us who are believers, this means that we are called not only to active commitment but also to constant prayer and the loving, patient perseverance that holds fast to faith in God's covenant and trusts in the Spirit working in human hearts and lives.

The Christian community has now existed for nearly 2,000 years and we can look back on a history not only of love and witness but also of continuous denial of the truths of the gospel and terrible evils done in the name of Jesus Christ. Can Christians, then, afford to cast stones at Marxists who have been attempting to liberate humanity for only the last 100 years? We have to take the plank out of our own eye before we can see to take the splinter out of our brother's eye. (Matt. 7:5) But the tragic experience of Stalinism and related evils have led a number of Marxists to appreciate the teaching of the gospel about such things as the wickedness of elitism, the abuse of power and the need for commitment and personal integrity. As Machovec puts it: 'Thus in the twentieth century, Marxists have painfully discovered how easily a one-sided stress on the paradise to come, which alone would be a genuinely human society, can lead to a fanaticism which abuses and ill-treats the present day members of society. Christians have often had similar experiences in the history of their movement.' [33]

We all know that the struggle to be more truthful, loving, fully human is not guaranteed for oneself, or others, by joining a church or a political party. In all existing human organisations we can find selfish pursuit of power; petty tyranny, spite and injustice; resort to lies and slander; contempt for the weak. But this does not mean that we are justified in withdrawing into despairing isolation. In these situations, Marxists, as Machovec again points out, see that 'their own experience of life now teaches them that there are many situations in which they must suffer injustice rather than contriubte to it. In this way they stand on a threshold where the deepest mystery of the New Testament no longer appears as mythology but as a profound and highly relevant truth.' [34] Do all Christians see that truth so clearly?

We need first to remind Marxists of their socialist ideals and Christians of their commitment to the gospel, and then we can speak to Marxists about the revolutionary character of true Christianity and show Christians how the truths of the gospel are embodied in socialism. We need to awaken Christians to a commitment to this earth and its future, and to their fellow human beings; we have to awaken Marxists to the love and solidarity of God, to the power and truth of the cross, the blessed community of the saints and the joy of resurrection. Eventually we shall be led into the unity which is the promise and the fulfilment of the new age when Christ will have 'made the two into one and broken down the hostility . . . to unite them both in a single body and reconcile them with God.' (Eph. 2:14–17) It is by that hope we live and we shall not be disappointed.

This lecture was given in March, 1983.

References

1 R. H. Tawney, *Religion and the Rise of Capitalism*, Penguin, p 270.

2 *ibid* p 273.

3 *ibid* p 276.

4 *ibid* p 277.

5 Quoted by C. Hill in *The World Turned Upside Down*, p 107.

6 *ibid* p 129.

7 *op cit.*

8 K. Marx, *The Communism of the Rheinischer Beobachter* in Marx and Engels *On Religion*. Progess, p 74.

9 J. Woods, *The Sermon on the Mount and its application*, Jefferey Blef, 1963, p 36.

10 J. Moltmann, *The Theology of Hope*, SCM, p 196.

11 *ibid*, p 67.

12 Fidel Castro quoted by G. Gutierrez in *A Theology of Liberation*, Orbis p 123.

13 F. Engels, *Socialism: Utopian and Scientific*, Progress, p 55.

14 J. Miranda, *Marx and the Bible*, Orbis, p 296.

15 K. Marx, *The Critique of the Gotha Programme* in Marx and Engels, *On Historical Materialism* p 165.

16 Aquinas quoted Chevrot, *Les Beatitudes* p 53.

17 *op cit* p 48.

18 John Paul II, Encyclical on Human Work, *Laborem Exercens*, CTS p 51.

19 *ibid* p 53.

20 *ibid* p 54.

21 *ibid* p 47.

22 *ibid* p 25.

23 *ibid* p 41.

24 *ibid* p 27.

25 *op cit* p 280.

26 H. K. McArthur, *Understanding the Sermon on the Mount*, Epworth Press, p 145.

27 H. Camara, *The Desert is Fertile*, Sheed and Ward, p 13.

28 J. B. Metz, *Followers of Christ*, Burns Oates/Paulist Press p 78.

29 F. Engels, Introduction to K. Marx *Class struggles in France* in Marx and Engels *On Historical Materialism*, p 270.

30 M. Machovec, *A Marxist looks at Jesus*, DLT p 33.

31 J. Moltmann, *op cit* p 338.

32 L. Ragaz, quoted by W. S. Kisinger in *The Sermon on the Mount: a history of interpretation and bibliography*, The Scarecrow Press p 94.

33 Machovec, *op cit* p 36.

34 *ibid* p 34.

Cedric Mayson

Liberation and the wine skin business

A white African looks at the Kingdom of God in the west-northerly world

I greet you with the good news of the Basileia, the Kingdom of God. In the prevailing situation of cynicism and gloom, people in the west-northerly parts of earth are unaccustomed to handling joy and certainty and hope, and it would be easy to indulge in the luxury of our lust for bad news.

We could spend our time scrawling insulting graffiti on the walls of our age, deploring the modern cults of affluence, capitalism, consumerism and usury which Tawney exposed; or the false gods of anti-communism and growth and profit which our world worships; or mocking a society based on elitism, exploitation and excesses; or a culture which cultivates killing; or a set of creeds which ensure that our traditions will take precedence over the Word of God; or the conflicting religious denominations whose lack of resemblance to the Way of Jesus questions their legitimacy. But having named the devils, we shall now cast them out, lest wallowing in the mud of our times precludes us from receiving the pearls of the gospel.

A liberated theological zone

Against the reality of 20th century badness we can set another reality of 20th century goodnews because recent decades have established one of the most liberated theological zones in history. Not only has the opium of 19th century religion worn off, but also the chains of captivity which were thrown on the church sixteen centuries ago by Constantine have at last been loosened.

We have demythologised the scriptures, demystified theology, depatriarchalised ministry, defantasised piety, deromanticised heaven and decimated the church. All of this is good if it prevents the waste of vast energies providing an expensive life-support system for belief and practices which have long since lost their grip on real life.

God is no longer made in the image of the emperor Constantine, queen Victoria, the archbishop or the chairman of the Anglo-American Corporation. For, in our rediscovery of the 'Jesus before Christianity;' we have found that, 'God does not want to be served by us, he wants to serve us; he does not want to be given the highest possible rank and status in our society, he wants to take the lowest place and be without any rank or status; he does not want to be feared and obeyed, he wants to be recognised in the sufferings of the poor and the weak; he is not supremely indifferent and detached, he is irrevocably committed to the liberation of humankind, for he has chosen to identify himself with all people in a spirit of solidarity and compassion'.[1]

These liberated theological concepts have enabled us to discard many ideas which had become simply religious junk, accumulated over the centuries, some of which can be given an honoured place in the museum of memory and some of which must be deliberately dumped.

The Basileia

Above all else in this age of theological liberation we have declassified the *Basileia*. The usual translation of this phrase as the 'Kingdom of God' is full of unsatisfactory connotations in an age which suspects both royalty and paternalism, and the sense of 'Kingdom' as a place, either in heaven or on earth, is misleading. Basileia means the ruling power of God, the realm of God, a divine jurisdiction built into the nature of human society. In the earliest written records of Jesus, the Basileia is the constantly recurring theme, underlying his first announcement of his ministry, his teaching, parables and activities, to the promises of the end.

Jesus made it patently clear that his understanding of life could not be fitted into the accepted theological, religious, political, economic or social categories. The good news is not confined to personal salvation, or life after death, or faith healing, or ecclesiastical organisation, or growing wealth — it is good news of God's rule among earthlings.

The Basileia was what Jesus was all about, the astonishing good news that every part of human society is within God's realm, where his power works like yeast in flour to transform society and will ultimately triumph. Yet almost immediately this proclamation of the Kingdom was shrouded behind veils of secrecy, distortion and denial. Between the first generation synoptic gospels of Mark, Matthew and Luke, and the second generation writings of Paul and John, the Basileia practically disappears and, as Christianity fell into the control of the idolatrous, the only aspects of God's realm which were allowed utterance were, 'the transcendental kingdom in heaven, or the inner kingdom of religious experience, or the cataclysmic kingdom of the apocalypticists . . . or the ecclesiastical kingdom of church expansion.'[2] But the proclamation of *the political kingdom of a new social order*, the central concept from which the praxis of Jesus was derived, was hardly heard in the centuries which followed.

However, the reality of the Basileia was not dependent on its proclamation, and it emerged even when the doctrine was lost in secrecy. Tawney, in 1922, is repeatedly prompted by it. Discussing the attitudes which religious opinion may adopt towards the world of social institutions and economic relations, he says, 'It may at once accept and criticise, tolerate and amend, welcome the gross world of human appetites as the squalid scaffolding from amid which the life of the spirit must arise and insist that this also is the material of the Kingdom of God'.[3]

Discussing a standard of values, he says, 'It must be based on some conception of the requirements of human nature as a whole, to which the satisfaction of economic needs is evidently vital, but which demands the satisfaction of other needs as well'.[4] He regrets that the nonconformist churches, 'saw the world of business and society as a battlefield across which character could march triumphant to its goal, not as crude materials waiting the architect's hand to set them in their place as the foundations of the Kingdom of Heaven'.[5] The essence of the good news of the Basileia, which has been rediscovered in our day, is that, beneath all human effort to overthrow the powers of evil in the world and establish a society based upon justice and peace and love, there is a positive yeasting power at work in human society towards that end.

The realm of God is not something which competes with Marxism, the liberation movements, capitalism, socialism, or any other programme. It is the driving force towards freedom, justice and peace which rises up within them in judgment and promise, dooming and overturning that which is wrong, empowering and inspiring the positive and good. It is the prototype shaped already by the coming of the end product. Our struggle for liberation, to enact a world worth living in, is not a struggle against the odds, but a struggle to let the victory emerge; not a struggle to achieve the unattainable, but a struggle to receive the experiencable.

The Basileia is the spiritual and secular actuality behind Bonhoeffer's 'religionless Christianity'. The death mask of doctrine, and resignation to a hopeless world, are both filled with new life when faith senses that Tillich's 'ground of our being' is stirring beneath our feet. Human society is going to be liberated and our endeavours must be designed to realise this in commitment and hope.

The truth of the Kingdom has designs upon us and many begin to catch the goodnews in their hearts, or even tap it with their toes, before they have apprehended its meaning with their minds. 'Theology today has yet to digest this radical change from the ethical to the eschatalogical understanding of the Kingdom of God,' writes Pannenburg.[6] And, as Arias suggests: 'The multidimensional nature of the Kingdom will not let us take refuge in our favourite dichotomies that plague our internal debate concerning the "spiritual and material", the "individual and social", the "historical and eternal", "evangelism and social action", and so on. Participation in the dynamic Kingdom of God, which is in-breaking through history to its final consummation, may become the most creative experience to inspire new methods and means of sharing and incarnating the good news of the Kingdom in our generation.'[7]

This vision, which changes our concept of Christianity from the practise of an individualistic religion into a breathtaking world view of human life and history operating within the realm of God, is good news to the poor but often bad news to those brought up to ecclesiastical privilege. Pannenburg points out that, 'Precisely because the church mistakes itself for the present form of the Kingdom, God's rule has often had to manifest itself in the secular world outside, and frequently against, the church'.[8] So it is not surprising to find non-Christian Marxists like Machovec writing: 'This astonishing orientation towards the future which is not passively awaited as something foreign, but it is rather experienced as something lived in the present, as the source of meaning for human life, as inner satisfaction, strength and − as they called it − "faith": this is the basis of early Christianity.'[9] The ideas of Jesus are 'the projection of the vision of the Kingdom of God on the present'.[10]

He continues: 'The Marxist stress on the future has provided new assumptions for the understanding of the eschatalogical-prophetic phenomenon in ancient Jewish and especially early Christian tradition'.[11] 'Many Marxists, but also many self-

critical modern theologians, are aware of the fact that concern for the future —
that longing for liberation and radical change once found in Christianity — has been
taken over in the modern period almost exclusively by Marxism.' [12] Christians
who find such an assertion somewhat affronting would do well to remember
Tawney's famous comment that the last of the schoolmen was Karl Marx rather
than Aquinas! [13]

Consideration of Christian belief in the Kingdom sets our feet well and truly into
the liberated zone of modern theology but, if we wish to study it further, the main
object of our research is not the Bible. The idea of the Kingdom, according to Pixley, 'has no existence in its purity and abstraction. It must always find expression
in some particular historical project, a project that may well exclude other projects
that also claim to embody the Kingdom of God'. [14]

We must examine the Basileia where it has been emerging in the world. Just as
those who sought to discover personal salvation went to the most godforsaken
experience they could imagine, the crucifixion, so we shall take our study of social
salvation to a godforsaken experience — South Africa.

The parable

This study may be captured in a succinct little parable of Jesus: 'Nobody puts new
wine into old wine skins: if they do, the wine will burst the skins and the wine
is lost and the skins too. No! New wine, new skins!' (Mark 2:21). The new vintage
of the Kingdom is the fresh harvest for humankind and it must be poured into new
wine skins: new thought forms, new ways for society, new methodologies. Neither
the old wine nor the old wine skins can contain the good news: it is a new message
demanding new structures.

We South Africans cannot tell you how to liberate yourselves, anymore than you
can tell us how to liberate ourselves, but with the insights of the kingdom, in either
Christian or Marxist terms or both, we are aware of the world-wide nature of the
struggle within human society. In some ways South Africa can serve as a model
because it is so much nearer liberation than Britain.

The people of South Africa are convinced that a new, liberated society is going
to emerge among them and they are totally committed to it. This faith feeds their
thinking, their actions and their exuberant spirits. It has prompted the 70-year-old
struggle of the African National Congress; was spelt out in the Freedom Charter;
was summarised in the United Democratic Front declaration for a united, non-
racial, democratic South Africa. Their commitment is demonstrated in the
protracted struggle to pull the tyrants from their thrones and by the willingness to
die for their faith. The South African army and police have realised the oppressor's
moment of truth, that weapons can achieve nothing against people who are willing
to lay down their lives for the Kingdom.

The contrast with the west-northerly countries could hardly be more marked.
Here, there is no widespread belief in, or expectation of, a new society or a commit-
ment to it. That need not deter you — you are simply at an earlier stage in the
process. Jesus had only 12 disciples and some of them were a bit shaky! In South
Africa there is a small nucleus with a vision of a new way, and some of them are
Christians and socialists. What can South Africa teach us of the wine skin business?

What new structures of thought and praxis have emerged in the quest for liberation?

It is convenient to examine this evidence in five areas of the Kingdom of God: the politics of the Kingdom in democracy; the economics of the Kingdom in terms of socialism; the ecology of the Kingdom as an holistic concept; the culture of the Kingdom as community; the personal acceptance of the Kingdom through faith.

The political liberation

The political liberation of the Kingdom of God in South Africa depends entirely upon the people: it is a democratic struggle. It is not being led by an elite in parliament, the church, the universities, enlightened business or political parties, but by uprising pressure from a highly politicised population. It is only within the masses of the ordinary people who suffer from it that the correct analysis of oppression can be made and the strategies of liberation be devised. Leadership is thrust up from the people to fulfil the will of the people. The government, which thinks solely in west-northerly terms of power imposed from the top, simply cannot understand how the struggle persists when they have spent years in picking off the leadership by banning, detention or murder. Elites can be destroyed, but the bottom is inexhaustible.

It was not always so. Our people were once as indoctrinated to accept their political dependency as the west-northerly people of today. But the deliberate policy of Steve Biko and his comrades in the Black Consciousness Movement changed that once and for all. Many of them were intellectuals but their skills were directed to the development of the consciousness they found in the ordinary people. Their leadership position was used not for their own aggrandisement but to plough back power into the grassroots. They liberated 'the theory class' by putting it in the control of the pragmatists: they had never heard of Gramsci but could recognise their gut feelings when they were spelt out by those with the gifts to write political programmes.

That process was taken further after the great bannings of 1977, when the whole liberation movement dived underground and throughout the country people mobilised one another about the vibrant issues which concerned them: high rents, bus fares, the need for school committees, decent wages, proper sewers and a hundred grassroot matters. Most had never heard of Lenin but, when the United Democratic Front was formed in 1983, tens of thousands of people in hundreds of small, local organisations put their concerns together in demands for fundamental national political change that reflected the earlier Freedom Charter and were both incisive and insatiable.

Change does not come from the top: it comes from a commitment to participatory democracy at the bottom. Though many of our people had not heard that Jesus said so, they were quite convinced that the Kingdom was among them, not far above them.

To an outsider it seems that most of the effort spent on political work in the west-northerly countries is directed towards achieving change from the top, by revitalising the old wine skins, and it does not work that way. Liberation is rooted downwards into the poor and dispossessed: the unemployed, children, women, the elderly, punks, blacks and those who feel their situation is hopeless. We must go to the godforsaken to hear the voice of God.

The changes demanded by the Kingdom are so fundamental that in our South African configuration we have rejected political parties as being irrelevant at this stage. We have opted for a liberation movement which unites people from many different backgrounds in a concerted effort to achieve the fundamental changes required in our quest for total national liberation. The leader of the opposition in the South African parliament recently walked out of parliament because he found it irrelevant to the quest of a new South Africa. Many third world observers of the west-northerly scene wonder if your political structures are truly relevant to the actual world situation, or if you are still trying to patch up the old wine skins.

The economic liberation

The economic liberation of the Kingdom of God in South Africa means socialism. Tawney wrote: 'The quality of modern societies which is most sharply opposed to the teaching ascribed to the founder of the Christian faith . . . consists in the assumption, accepted by most reformers with hardly less naivete than by defenders of the estalished order, that the attainment of material riches is the supreme object of human endeavour and the final criterion of human success . . . It is the negation of any system of thought or morals which can, except by a metaphor, be described as Christian. Compromise is as impossible between the church of Christ and the idolatory of wealth, which is the practical religion of capitalist societies, as it was between the church and the state idolatory of the Roman empire.' [15]

Two aspects of the South African struggle may be mentioned here. The moral and theological justification of apartheid has been declared a heresy by nearly all of Christendom, which views the doctrine with such abhorrence that its adherents must recant their views before they can be accepted into the Christian community. To what extent is the failure of the west-northerly Christians to denounce as heresy the moral and theological justification of capitalism a sign of decadence, a clinging to the old wine skins which exactly matches the attitude of the Dutch Reformed Church to apartheid?

The greatest danger to Christianity is not from those who deny it, but from those who hereticise it. Religious people become heretics. They would like to see a few reforms but the last thing many of them want is the Kingdom of God on earth.

And reform is not an option in South Africa. Our people are convinced there is no way in which a society centred on and ruled by rich capitalists, who maintain their position only by violence, can be changed gradually and gently into a society in which people shall govern and the land and wealth be shared by all. You cannot worship God and mammon, and it is simply absurd to image that the devil will bring the Kingdom of God on earth if you ask him nicely. The economic base of the Kingdom of God can only be discovered when the capitalist system is overthrown and the socialist system deliberately embraced. Socialism must be given a preferential position on the Christian agenda. But Desmond reminds us that, 'Socialism does not provide a solution for the problems of South Africa . . . in the sense that somewhere . . . there is a blueprint which, given a bit of goodwill on all sides, could be implemented in South Africa. A solution cannot be found: it can only be worked out: and socialism provides the framework for doing that'.[16]

The ecology of the Kingdom

The ecology of the Kingdom is a wide subject bringing all material things into a holistic unity. Much of it is related to the land issue, not only its treatment but also its ownership. Earthlings on this land which God found good will live inhuman lives unless they have land to live on. The Kingdom cannot accept the system in South Africa whereby 85 per cent of the population are condemned to live on 13 per cent of the land. Can it accept the system in the west-northerly countries where 90 per cent of the land is owned by 5 per cent of the population, or some slight variant, and whereby the wealthy price land so highly that a family must spend nearly a third of their income to keep a roof over their heads?

The culture of the Kingdom

The culture of the Kindom embraces the breadth of human communities. The difficulties of discovering how people of different backgrounds can live together are rewarded by the unexpected richness of their experience when they do. That is something which has been discovered in the non-racial experience of South Africans whenever they have ventured into it, particularly in the liberation movements.

The churches, despite their provision of some centres for the discovery of a Kingdom culture, are doomed by their present structures, and in great need of cultural liberation. West suggests that, 'class struggle is not simply the battle between capitalists and the proletariat, owners and producers in the work situation. It also takes the form of cultural and religious conflict over which attitudes, values, and beliefs will dominate the thought and behaviours of people.'[17] The church needs a revolution to liberate it. It has too frequently aligned itself with the oppressive structures and modelled itself upon them. It is concerned for the poor, but supports the systems that make people poor. It advocates charity but tolerates injustice. The Revd Barney Pityana has written, 'The churches seek to win concessions from oppressive systems instead of seeking to change those systems.'[18]

Church folk make desperate attempts to remodel the old ecclesiastical wineskins to hold the new wine of the Kingdom, many even grasping the new liberating theologies in the hope they will put new life into the church! They are not bothered about the wine, but the wine skins! The British public, frequently confronted by hoardings requesting them to HELP RENOVATE THIS MEDIAEVAL CHURCH know the appeal is not limited to the fabric of the building.

Wherever the Kingdom has been breaking through, new forms of church have come into being. There are several hundred thousand base communities in South America. The Kairos Document, which was born in Soweto and is revolutionising churches throughout South Africa — to say nothing of the astonishing demand for it from the world outside, came from a small group of Christian people seeking to respond to the crisis of their times. Liberation does not emanate from the official structures of the church. 'Theology is challenged by the sad appearance of the empirical church as a hangover from another historical period,' writes Pannenburg.

'The appropriate response to this challenge is to be found in a new emphasis upon the church as an eschatalogical community pioneering the future of all people.'[19]

There seems to be no doubt that this is happening in South Africa, where a new church movement is recognisable among Christians who have become involved in the liberation struggle. This phenomenon first became prominent in the Christian Institute which the government banned in 1977, forgetting the resurrection assurance of a 'sorceror's magician' effect upon any attempt to kill the Kingdom. Since then there has been a proliferation of Christian people involved in the struggle at all levels.

Migues Bonino observed that, 'A social location determines a perspective'.[20] Christians who locate themselves in the struggle for liberation discover a new way of looking at life, relating to one another and being the church. It is when they do this together that liberation begins to enculture their experience.

Part of their problem is to keep their priorities clear. Pannenburg has pointed out that, 'the theological identification of the church with the Kingdom of Christ has all too often served the purposes of ecclesiastical officials who are not attuned to the Kingdom of God'.[21] This should not distract us unduly. Our main task is not to radicalise the church but to reinforce the liberation struggle in the world. Jesus never sent his followers to convert the religious conservatives: 'Leave them alone,' was his advice.

Writing inside South Africa before he was killed, Rick Turner wrote: 'The majority of church leaders seem content to continue to operate within the framework of the status quo and see Christianity as an internal morality rather than a transcendent morality that challenges the status quo'.[22] There is no way in which a liberated Christian culture can be built within such a church. The new wine must go into the new wine skins. What that means in the exigencies of the struggle in South Africa today is that the Christian initiative is held by small, informal groups of Christians. What it means for the church in the long run will emerge. What it means for the church in the west-northerlies is for you to discover: but you can forget the old wine skins.

Faith in the Kingdom

Personal faith in the Kingdom is the fifth and final aspect of the liberation struggle, the emergence of a life-changing belief. 'A capitalist society survives largely because . . . most individuals do not know that any other form of society is possible.'[23] Oppressive regimes continue to grow because their roots are not seriously disturbed and because they exercise such a stranglehold of power upon the means of communication and normal human experience that people are warped without knowing it, oppressed without recognising that they are chained, not suspecting that the cancer of fascism and capitalism is rampant and destructive within their society. As Tawney puts it: 'There is a moral and religious, as well as a material, environment, which sets its stamp on the individuals, even when they are least conscious of it'.[24]

It is in this area that conversion becomes vital, that the process which is referred to by president Canaan Banana as 'cultural and psychological decolonisation' takes place. The key element for Christians is what it always has been − proclaiming the goodnews of the Kingdom. There is a task for politicians in liberation; a task for economists; a task for propagandists and freedom fighters and every sort of activist; but the peculiar task of promoting the liberation faith is the task of evangelists.

Politicians politicise it; economists plan it; propagandists publicise it; guerillas fight for it; and evangelists proclaim it. That is what the Kairos Document does in South Africa. Evangelism does not mean offering people, as an emotional fizzbang, some heavenly encouragement to cop out of the struggle. It means offering people the experience of belief, of recognising the transcendent reality most call God in the context of today's world. 'By witnessing to the future fulfilment of humanity in God's Kingdom,' Pannenburg writes, 'the church helps to stir the imagination for social action and to inspire the visions of social change. In a time when many intelligent people doubt that humankind has a future, the church must more urgently and persuasively proclaim the Kingdom of God.' [25]

Old time evangelists urged sinners to turn from their sinful ways and receive a new life, and that is what happens today: indeed, the people long to hear the herald's sound. Turn away from the false gods of west-northernism, give up your addiction to the media which corrupts your thinking and your morals, shake off the burden of running church activities which have nothing to do with the Kingdom and put your whole heart into those that do. Throw away your obsession with converting rightwing religious people and find your allies where Jesus did, in the workplace and the homes of the people, break out of your dependence on false life styles and your acceptance of evil regimes. The Kingdom is at hand: go for it!

'Faith makes the Christian someone who, within history, sides with God's intentions for his creation against the tyrants who, in their madness, want to destroy the earth and its inhabitants. Faith sees that god is the living one whose supremacy is final.'[26] Thus testifies Allan Boesak. One of the things we have discovered in the South African struggle is the great unhappiness of those who stick in the negative rut of being against apartheid. Those who find the exuberant experience of the Kingdom becoming real in themselves are those who commit themselves very positively to the liberation struggle.

That act of faith is sealed, not by kneeling at the penitents' bench, but by linking arms with your comrades. In that good news I greet you.

This lecture was given in March, 1986.

References

1 A. Nolan, *Jesus before Christianity*, 1976, p 137.

2 M. Arias, *Announcing the Reign of God; Evangelisation and the Subversive Memory of Jesus*, 1984, p xv.

3 R. H. Tawney, *Religion and the Rise of Capitalism* (1922), 1926 (references to the 1961 Pelican edition), p 30.

4 ibid p 277.

5 ibid p 275.

6 W. Pannenburg, *Theology and the Kingdom of God*, 1969, p 78.

7 Arias, op cit, p xvii.

8 Pannenburg, op cit, p 78.

9 M. Machovec, *A Marxist Looks at Jesus* (1972), 1976, p 90.

10 ibid p 201.

11 ibid p 214.

12 ibid p 193.

13 Tawney op cit, p 48.

14 G. V. Pixley, *God's Kingdom*, 1981, p 2.

15 Tawney, op cit, p 280.

16 C. Desmond, *Christians or Capitalists? Christianity and Politics in South Africa*, 1978, p 134.

17 C. West, *Prophesy Deliverance*, 1982, p 118.

18 B. Pityana, *Index on Censorship*, May 1983.

19 Pannenburg, op cit, p 75.

20 M. Bonino, *Towards a Christian Political Ethics*, 1983, p 43.

21 Pannenburg, op cit, p 78.

22 R. Turner, *The Eye of the Needle*, 1972, p 138.

23 ibid p 51.

24 Tawney, op cit, p 26.

25 Pannenburg, op cit, p 85.

26 A. Boesak, *The Finger of God*, 1982, p 35.

Charles Elliott
A view from the underside

The critique of British economic management that would be offered by Christians in other parts of the world

I must begin by explaining why I choose to speak on this topic. There are several reasons. The technocratic tradition has long been that we in the UK or the US have a natural right to comment freely and adversely on the mess, as we usually see it, that developing countries make of running their economies. Behind this lie the thin assumptions that (a) we have superior knowledge, judgment and wisdom in these matters and it therefore behoves us to share them with our ignorant colleagues overseas; and (b) we have a duty to put them right, a latter day obligation to assume the white man's burden. Both of these assumptions are such twaddle that I thought it might at least be healthy to stand the process on its head. Rather than tell the Argentinians, the Mexicans or the Zambians what a terrible mess they make of things – and in those countries at least there would be some excuse for starting from that position – let us try to hear what people from those countries, or other countries in the developing world, might have to say to us as they contemplate the recent economic history of this country. Let us, in other words, take a little of our own medicine.

There is a case for saying that the UK is approaching the status and structure of a developing country itself. It is, no doubt, still a relatively rich developing country but, in terms of structure, there are some striking analogies. Unemployment in some parts of urban Britain, up to 80 per cent, is actually higher than in many third world cities. The proportion of GDP accounted for by manufactures is now not much different from many of the more industrialised, middle-income countries. The co-existence, often over a small area, of private affluence and public squalor is reminiscent of Latin America and the chronic machismo, which afflicts British consumers of all sorts, is identical to what you find in many countries of that great continent. Our class structure is, so we imagine, uniquely British but, in its rigidity, its effect on economic and political life, its incompatibility with a major redistribution of income, wealth and power it has in fact many similarities with countries saddled with the relics of a colonial, landed oligarchy. Even the churches remind me of Latin America. In their essence, chaplains to the establishment and the status quo, they boast at best rebellious fringes, often wholly marginalised, trying to live and proclaim a truer gospel.

If there is anything in this idea of Britain as a developing – or, to use a more accurate vocabulary, underdeveloped − country, then it clearly makes sense to have a look at our predicament through the eyes of those who share it.

But why, you may ask, concentrate on economic management? Why not look at our whole social situation? For underdevelopment is a much wider, perhaps even much more interesting, phenomenon than economic management. I want to concentrate (more or less) on management because I believe it offers us an unusually good litmus test of the values, priorities, assumptions and world-views of those who make key decisions. If we want to know more about the form and nature of our peculiar variety of underdevelopment, such variables will be especially helpful.

I chose to reflect on what Christians from the third world are saying about our economic management − rather than, for instance, economic technocrats − because I want to develop a recognisably Christian critique of our situation. And I chose Christians from the third world because many of them have had to plumb the depth of their faith to make difficult existential decisions in a way that few people in the UK ever have to. I refer not to the much publicised issue of whether to use violence against the state, a key decision for many faithful Christians in South Africa, central America and the Philippines, but to the more mundane issues of living as a spiritual, political and economic animal in a society in which the structural deformities are so glaring, so burdensome to the poor and so corrupting to the rich, that ultimate questions of identity, meaning and relationship inevitably burst through the surface of faith. I suspect our fellow Christians in such an environment may see things more clearly, more trenchantly, than we can. At least they are not blinkered by convention and familiarity.

Method

So much by way of explanation − and apology − for this slightly bizarre topic. Now I must say a brief word about method. What I shall try to present to you can lay no claims to scientific objectivity. It results from no formal fieldwork but is based on long conversations I have had over the last months with fellow Christians, who happen to be professional economists, from Bangladesh, Nicaragua, Kenya and Brazil. All are, to a greater or lesser degree, familiar with the UK scene and all have an affection, not always untinged with its opposite, for this country.

So what would they want us to hear if they were here? They would not, of course, use the same vocabulary, the same analytical methods or the same political or theological assumptions. Nor would they agree on every point. I have, however, been impressed by the general consensus that seems to emerge from my conversations with them.

You will have noticed immediately that two of the four countries are extremely poor; that one is going through a major crisis brought about by external factors; and one is in a precarious financial and therefore political position. In all four, though for different reasons, economists in general and Christian economists in particular are being forced back to the most basic questions about the nature and purpose of economic activity, and especially of economic growth. One form in which this line of questioning presents itself is this: what is the trade off between consumption today and more consumption the day after tomorrow? How much consumption is it proper to forego today in order to have more consumption in five years time?

Traditionally the answer has tended to be determined by political processes rather than by straight economic technique. And that is as it should be, for economics cannot answer what are essentially questions of value. Nonetheless, the *bias* of economics has been to press for less consumption today; more savings; more investment − in the hope of higher consumption for the next generation.

Now the people I talk to in the four countries I mentioned are beginning to wonder whether the traditional bias, with its roots in Harrod-Domar type thinking about growth processes, is not due for a fundamental re-examination. They are asking that not from the perspectives we are familiar with, the Club of Rome limits-to-growth argument, that finite resources cannot support infinite consumption. Nor from a natural, if grim, assumption that as the probability of nuclear holocaust rises, the arguments for investing in the future diminish. Their call for a re-examination of economic growth fetishism comes from a much more mundane but a more deeply Christian concern for the present victims of the cost of economic growth.

There are in fact two rather different ways of developing the argument and it is important to keep them separate. The first development is to say that when people are already on the poverty line in absolute terms, it is morally unacceptable to give *any* weight to *increases* in consumption in the future. (Increases in population are a slight complicating factor but they can be ignored for ease of exposition.) Therefore, so this form of argument goes, available resources should not be pre-empted for investment but should be used to raise levels of consumption among the poorest until they reach an 'acceptable' level. (That raises some interesting arguments about what, precisely, that means, but we can leave that aside.) Only when the consumption of everyone has reached such a level should additional resources be put into net investment.

The difficulty with this crude formulation in all four countries − and most obviously in Bangladesh − is that if there is no net investment there will never be sufficient resources to give all 100 million people an 'acceptable' level of living. There simply is not enough to go round if it were spread equally and there were no diversion of resources to investment.

That is why the more subtle formulation, most thoroughly worked out in Nicaragua for obvious reasons, is concerned not with foregoing all growth but, rather, asking much more serious questions about the *nature* of growth, the content and output of investment and the distribution of the product. This neo-Ricardian approach seeks to ensure that consumption foregone, represented by investment, raises the real wages of the poorest by increasing the supply and/or reducing the price of wage-goods; by raising employment, especially of unskilled workers; and by increasing the supply of low-tech inputs for farmers and artisans. In other words, growth is not forsaken, but a much more deliberate attempt is made to ensure that the nature of the growth responds to the needs of the poorest. It is made to serve them; rather than the reverse.

Recent British experience

This is particularly relevant when these people reflect on the British experience, especially since 1979. They express surprise and dismay that none of this thinking seems to be reflected in our own policies at a time when one family in eight is living on supplementary benefit. What is the point, they ask, of a form of economic growth that produces unemployment, raises direct and indirect taxes and does nothing to reduce the prices of wage-goods? That is to extort a high cost from the poorest for a form of growth that will benefit neither them nor their children.

If we reply that we are obliged to follow the patterns of growth determined by our trading partners and especially the technological leaders — for if we go our own way, we shall be unable to compete in world markets — my third world friends look sceptical. They agree that, as long as we are structurally bound to the US and continental Europe, we make things more difficult for ourselves but they argue that, even within those admitted constraints, we are not obliged to remain entirely passive to the sources and form of growth that takes place. They put it more sharply: should there be no social control on the use of investment resources when unemployment is high; when capital/labour ratios are variable but can be very high; and when import penetration of the wage-goods sector is so far advanced? 'Your unemployment/low growth/weak balance of payments problem,' they say, 'is entirely of your own making. You invest too little at home; in the wrong things; with the wrong technology and leave the wage-goods sector wide open to imports.'

Seen from the perspective of the third world our failure to use our savings in ways more directly related to our social needs seems puzzling to the point of perversity — a judgment raised to a higher power by the liberality with which our savings are invested overseas, often to the direct benefit of our foreign competitors in our own domestic market. It is hard to exaggerate the bewilderment with which observers from the third world watch what is going on. 'You're mad,' was the summary judgment of a Brazilian friend.

Are we mad? Perhaps we are infected with the madness of history. Caught on the cusp of our rise and fall as an industrial nation, we are deluded by the afterglow of past grandeur into thinking that we can operate a free market economy in a way that will, sooner or later, spread its benefits throughout society. Such a delusion makes so many false assumptions I cannot enumerate them all here. My aim is more modest: to report that third world observers cannot understand why we tolerate structural unemployment of four million and simultaneously take so little interest in the way investible resources are actually used.

They also wonder, along the lines of the 'crude' version of the argument, why we lend resources to foreigners at a time when so large a proportion of our own population lives on the poverty line. 'If you didn't *need* the resources yourselves,' said a Kenyan, 'I could understand what you were doing. But you save what you can and then turn your back on your own people. How can that be right?'

At one level, of course, such questions are very naive. At another — a more human or, if you like, a more spiritual — they are profound indeed. Many third world Christians take it as an unspoken assumption that the whole community has a responsibility for all people within it. To them any form of economic organisation that cuts across that assumption needs to be brought under the judgment of God. Thus the fact that savings are owned by the comfortable classes who want to protect the comfort of the next generation is, in their eyes, not a sufficient reason for denying access to them to those whose needs, for both consumption and investment, are pressing. I am not implying that all third world Christians are natural socialists: you don't have to spend long in Kenya or Brazil to see that! I am saying that when they have managed to avoid the extreme individualism that has too often accompanied the proclamation of the Christian faith, they see our situation with an undiluted sharpness that pushes us back to questioning priorities. Are we putting too much emphasis on more jam tomorrow? Do we *really* need growth at the cost of six million people living in poverty. Can't we design a style of growth that gives first priority to meeting the basic needs of poor families?

Economic strategies

It is beyond my remit to give instant answers to those questions but I cannot escape one or two quick comments. Clearly the last question is the most fundamental. What does it imply about economic strategy? The issue is far deeper than current discussions about the budget, the poverty trap or the structure of benefits. It is rather about the way in which any society can control or at least influence the style of growth, that is the pattern of investment, the structure of demand and nature of technology. There is, of course, as a recent issue of the *New Statesman* attests, currently a major debate raging about this very issue. For myself, especially as I hear friends from the third world, I cannot conceive how social control can be exercised on those critical questions without major and direct state intervention. The modalities of that intervention — whether through large scale public ownership; investment accords; minority shareholdings or Japanese-style interaction between large private companies and a highly directive (albeit informally directive) state apparatus — are questions for subsequent discussion. What is clear, however, is that significant increases in the earned incomes of poor people can only be achieved if the state accepts responsibility for monitoring and, if necessary, controlling the *style* of economic growth and not only its rate.

Secondly, our third world friends, truer perhaps to the Ricardian tradition than we, ask us to look with fresh eyes on what has vulgarly come to be known as supply side economics. As interpreted in the US, this has been associated with a highly regressive trend in income distribution — a trend reflected here, too, as the recent article by Morris and Preston in *Fiscal Studies* has demonstrated beyond any further doubt. That is, however, only one variety of supply side economics. A variant is to look at the supply and the market conditions of that supply of wage-goods. We may need to ask, for example, how it comes about that the price of luxury goods has risen in real terms much less than wage-goods. To give one or two examples: over the last 30 years the cost of Scotch has risen less than five-fold; of beer more than eleven-fold; the cost of bread has risen fifteen-fold while the cost of a return airfare to Paris only ten-fold. As a recent article in *Which* showed, in nearly every case of wage-goods that they researched, the current price is higher than inflation in the 30-year period would explain. This strongly suggests that the supply of non-wage-goods (luxury items and household durables) has been more cost-saving than that of wage-goods. There is a whole battery of reasons why that should be so, from changes in technology to the market power of leading suppliers, and it is beyond my purpose to review them here. I can only reflect that people in the developing world, who have had to think hard about the so-called basic needs approach to development, deserve a careful hearing when they tell us that one aspect of the style of growth that needs special attention is the supply of wage-goods.

The distribution of wealth and power

I want now to move on to a related topic — namely the distribution of wealth and, associated weakly with that, of economic power. I hear Christian economists in the developing world deeply troubled by the tendency of western styles of development, which, with more or less local adaptation, they have adopted, to polarise society with respect to income, wealth and power. One only has to spend a few days in Nairobi or Sao Paulo or, in a quite different key, Dhaka to see the outward and visible signs of enormous inequalities in wealth. But it is less the fact of inequality itself than the effect such inequalities have on the distribution of power within society that worries third world observers. This is not only a question of corruption: though that has become a major source of political instability in both Kenya and Bangladesh. Much more, it is also the fear that the legitimate government finds its room for manoeuvre constantly constricted by the economic power and political connections of a relatively small, often highly inter-connected, group of ultra-wealthy individuals.

When they look at the UK, they see the same processes at work, with the additional complication that economic power is wielded not only by the ultra-wealthy but also by the managers of aggregations of wealth — the insurance companies, pension funds and financial institutions. The issue is not only whether the power of such people is used benignly or not but also, whether it is consistent with democratic values at all.

My friends would have no difficulty in citing chapter and verse for their concern. Every survey that has ever been carried out on the wishes of the British people shows that the vast majority think that the overseas aid programme should be structured in a way that enables poor people to help themsleves. But the present government, building, it has to be said, on a foundation left by the last Labour administration, has used an increasing proportion of the aid vote to subsidise British exporters. Not only has it greatly expanded the aid trade provision within a smaller aid programme, but it has also begun to raid the 'normal' bilateral programme for funds to subsidise either the direct cost or the credit-cost of export deals. It is hard for detached observers — who see the outcome of these processes in the shape, for example, of the disastrous Sicartsa Steel Works in Mexico — to suppress the thought that what keeps in being a programme that has been heavily criticised by the treasury and the independent evaluators appointed by the government is pressure from the beneficiaries and their would-be allies. Perhaps they see our world through eyes familiar with a different landscape. Perhaps. And perhaps such eyes see with the greater clarity.

This form of distortion in economic priorities is, however, only a pimple on the body politic. Much more significant is the capacity of the wealthy and their international allies to determine the parameters of political debate. In the developing world very crude means are adopted to ensure that — martial law in Bangladesh, censorship in Kenya, terror in Brazil's recent past. My third world friends are not deceived by our greater sophistication. They look not only at the control and crypto-control of the mass media — revealing though that may be — but also at the much more insidious mechanisms that stem from the globalisation of the world's capital markets and the internationalisation of production through transnational corporations. The effect, they surmise, is to reduce any government's freedom of action by threats of capital flight, speculation against sterling, the transfer of production and the cessation of technology transfer. Faced with those kinds of risks, which follow directly from the concentration of economic power, the options available to a government are curtailed; the range of political discourse is limited.

To this extent, a recent report in the *Financial Times* would cause my third world colleagues no surprise. This is what is had to say: 'Top Japanese industrial executives yesterday stepped up their threats to reduce investment in Europe and close down European factories if a controversial EEC proposal to extend anti-dumping duties is approved.' (March 5, 1987)

Many developing countries themselves have been the victims of exactly that kind of pressure, but third world economists now emphasise the link between domestic capital and the so-called comprador class on the one hand and international capital on the other. The nature and effects of those links are, of course, much diluted, but looking at the UK, observers from the developing world wonder whether we are now, in this respect, in any better a position than they are. They wonder if it is not already too late; if the processes by which the UK is neutered politically have not now gone so far as to be irreversible. They wonder, indeed, whether Mrs Thatcher really needs a third term in office to exterminate socialism. Reflecting on Chile, Jamaica, Pakistan and Peru, they are perhaps more anxious than we are that the combination of the concentration of domestic wealth with the globalisation of economic and financial resources makes talk of political freedom hollow indeed.

I want to conclude this section with a more low-key footnote. It is a point so obvious that it has to be included more for completeness than for illumination. It is the matter of tribalism. My African friends tell me they feel increasingly at home in Britain because they recognise even more clearly the emergence – perhaps one ought to say re-emergence – of the British equivalent of tribalism. There are the familiar gaps between north and south; Wales and south England; highlands of Scotland and midlands of England. These distinctions have increased, are increasing and ought to be diminished. They are related to issues of income distribution and wealth concentration to which I have already referred. We have, also, a relatively new brand of tribalism: yuppies, dinkies and sehos. What my African friends find hard to understand is why any government would give these already prosperous tribes so many additional fiscal advantages – mortgage relief; pension relief; tax free perks; subsidised private health care and education. 'If the Kikuyu got that lot,' said a Kenyan friend, 'they would rise in rebellion'. I make the point lightly: but our social and economic divisions are a weighty matter – and to none more than to Christians who take seriously Pauline body-imagery with respect to community.

Education and social welfare

Another area of great interest to third world economists, and perhaps especially to those with a faith dimension to their professional involvement, is what is known in the trade as human resource development – education, training, health care, housing. As with growth theory, so with the theory of human resource development: there is a large literature, a series of anguished debates and no final conclusion. The most central debates are two: quantity v quality and social demand v economic demand. Clearly the two are related. If you go for social demand for education, in virtually any developing country, you are committed to quantity, and quality will have to look after itself. Nonetheless, bitter experience in each of the four countries I have mentioned – Brazil, Bangladesh, Kenya and Nicaragua – has forced questions of quality higher and higher on the agenda. In situations of extreme resource scarcity, much creative thinking has gone into discovering means by which quality may be raised without compromising the commitment to expand quantity. This kind of approach revolutionised the whole conception of health care in Nicaragua, producing a model of upstream focussing that emphasises prevention and promotion and which has become a favourite of the World Health Organisation in its campaign of Health for All by 2000. The success of the Nicaraguan literacy campaign, innovative to the point of high-risk as it was, is well known. Not surprisingly the other three countries have produced less revolutionary ideas. But even Bangladesh has taken a major step forward in improving local drug supply at prices people can afford and is on the brink of launching the biggest, and in some ways most innovative, literacy campaign in the developing world.

From that background, my third world friends gasp with horror at the lack of creative imagination that is brought to bear on these areas in this country. It is easy to condemn the 'Thatcher cuts' and no one from the third world that I speak to can understand why a still wealthy Britain is so set on destroying its two greatest assets – its education system and the National Health Service. Let's leave that aside as common ground that needs no further exploration. The more interesting points they make are about our failure to adapt the *style* of our social services to our needs and our resources – even if those resources were much less heavily constrained than the present government has made them. Let me illustrate. Depression, industrial accidents, road accidents and smoking-related diseases account between them for nearly (on some estimates more than) half the running costs of our hospitals. They tend to be socially regressive in their incidence – though less so in their treatment (as many lower-income depressives go untreated, especially in hospital). All four groups are amenable to prevention and/or health promotion interventions at very low social cost. If, for example, fines for breaches of safety at work regulations were increased twenty-fold, it is hard to believe that industrial accidents would not diminish. If speed restrictions were enforced; driving and drinking banned; safety engineering of vehicles and roads made mandatory and pedestrian flows properly channelled, it is inconceivable that road accidents would not be reduced. More tricky in the short term, if our inner cities were less lonely, less violent and less miserable places to live – and that does not necessarily mean wholesale rebuilding – it is probable that depression, particularly among house or child-bound women, would be greatly reduced.

And what of education? That our schools are in crisis is a cliché. To third world visitors they come as a shock; almost an outrage. They see the problem, however, not only in terms of money; nor only in terms of money and political control. They are also astonished at the evaporation of our institutional creativity. We may not have invented the kindergarten, the school, the teacher training college and the university – but we developed each to a high degree of excellence and exported each all over the world. But as conditions have changed, so we seem to have got stuck with models that might have been appropriate for the nineteenth century but are becoming increasingly questionable in the twentieth — and will break down for sure in the twenty-first. They ask a harder question — and one that British socialists dislike. Is it, they say, that you have forgotten how to think creatively? Or is it that there are now so many vested interests around the health and education sectors that there is no point in thinking creatively? When we protest that there is no point in thinking creatively when there is no money to finance what we have already, they point out that it is precisely resource scarcity that made them think creatively. 'We may not have found perfect solutions,' said a Kenyan as he showed me round a Harambee school, 'but we have no alternative but to go on looking for one.'

We are, I believe, challenged deeply at this point. The right has made voluntarism, community care, parent involvement and de-institutionalisation not the energising search for new models to meet fundamental needs but, too often, a tawdry expedient for saving public expenditure. The easy reply is to cut short the search for new models and spend more money on the old models in an attempt to breathe new life into them. It may work. For my part, I would prefer to listen to what our friends overseas are saying and continue the hunt, not as a short cut to reduced expenditure, but as a recognition that different problems require different solutions.

The world economy

Two further areas can be described more briefly. The first relates to the international economy in general and commodity prices in particular. My third world colleagues are, of course, familiar with the destructive effects that the long downswing in commodity prices has had on their economies — and hardly less so the extreme volatility of those prices. Witness the recovery of the tea price 1985–86 and of coffee 1984–85. Short-term fluctuations are highly destabilising; long-term decline in the net barter terms of trade, a process that has been going on since 1951, is debilitating. The former may be unfortunate; the latter is unjust. The damage it has caused, not excluding much of the African famine of 1983–85, is incalculable.

Colleagues from the developing world had hoped that with the discovery of North Sea oil Britain would at least begin to see the absurdity of an international trading regime that relies wholly on the market. I avoid the usual epithet 'free' market because, with power so unevenly divided between buyers and sellers, commodity markets (with the possible exception of oil) are not free in any significant sense.

Rather in the same way as *The Church and the Bomb* managed to have its moral cake and eat it — by decrying British nuclear arms but depending on American ones — so we are seen as achieving the same duplicitous trick with respect to oil. We refuse to join OPEC but we rejoice when it manages, by cutting back its own production, to turn the price back towards $18 a barrel. Our third world critics see this as a way of holding a fig leaf of respectability over our refusal to take the commodity problem seriously — without even having to pay for the fig leaf. That the Tories behave in this way comes as no great surprise; that Roy Hattersley and the Labour Party take the same position — at an ODI meeting Mr Hattersley went on record as saying he had no ideas for an approach to the commodity problem — comes as a great disappointment. True, Britain has not the same interest in the oil price — if the treasury macro-model is to be believed — as, for example, Kenya has in coffee or Bangladesh, an extreme and even tragic case, has in jute. Precisely because she has *an* interest without being dominated by it, Britain could, say our friendly critics, play a particularly key role.

What could that role consist of? After much huffing and puffing and a report from a House of Commons select committee that even the *Economist* called 'damning', the Labour government did ratify the common fund, secure, one suspects, in the knowledge that there was no prospect whatever of the US Or Japan doing so. With the wisdom of hindsight one can see that with the onset of the global recession and the emergence of the new right, the common fund would have been shortlived, unhelpful and expensive. Sometimes, it seems, the sons of darkness get it right!

This is not the time or place to go into an extremely complex field: let me report only what I hear colleagues from the developing world say. They say this: 'You tried to do with your own primary producers, your farmers, what you quarter-try to do with global primary producers — that is, manage the market through the common agricultural policy. Even the French and Germans are now recognising what many sensible people in Britain, on both left and right, always suspected, that that won't work. No more will international commodity agreements, as we have found with tin, cocoa, sugar and coffee. The EEC, sensibly and humanely, is now realising that the only way farmers' incomes can be protected is by some form of income guarantee supplemented by production quotas. So let it be at the international level. We will tolerate production quotas if, but only if, there is some form of income guarantee.'

Personally I cannot understand how, morally, a principle that is applied to white European primary producers can be denied to black, third world primary producers. The latter of course have no votes in European politics, but to allow the arbitrary distribution of political influence to determine morality is not something either Christians or socialists would want to be known for.

Development and economic justice

My final topic is related to commodity prices — both for the developing world and for the UK As is well known, many developing country commodity exporters have been under great pressure from the IMF to devalue their currencies, in an effort to move productive resources into the export sector, and simultaneously to raise the price of imports. As is also well known, the distributional impact of these depreciations has been severe — hence the spate of bread riots culminating in the Copperbelt disturbances in Zambia at the end of last year.

Unsurprisingly, there is a strong critique of IMF orthodoxy emerging from the third world which centres on two propositions. First, in many countries imports have already been cut to the bone. Raising prices further merely fuels domestic inflation and/or impedes the recovery of industry and agriculture which are dependent upon imported inputs. Secondly, devaluation *per se* does nothing to expand demand for commodity exports. If it merely increases domestic supply it will, especially if replicated throughout the developing world, merely induce a further collapse in commodity prices.

Looking at our condition through the eyes of this experience and the debates it has sparked, Christian economists in the developing world wonder at the power of economic ideology. Their wonderment is much increased when they see that power demonstrated here by the mercifully short but wholly inglorious reign of monetarism — an episode that cost the poor of this country more than they yet realise. What is it, they ask, that gets into decision makers that induces them to follow a road that can only have the most negative effects. Why are they the seemingly willing victims of economic ideas that are clearly destructive?

They point out two parallels between their experience of IMF-type orthodoxy, which is a somewhat refined, somewhat coded form of monetarism, and the crude monetarism which we suffered from 1980 to 1984. First, the distributional impact is regressive, unanalysed and uncompensated, not least because the political and economic interests of those who impose the policies are either served (as in the UK case) or unaffected (as in some, but not all, developing countries). In other words, you cannot divorce consideration of the demonic nature of economic ideology from consideration of the demonic nature of the state. If the state has been hijacked by — or put in hock to — those who can afford, in every sense, to neglect the issue of social justice, *any* ideology that does not have justice at its centre is likely to damage the poor and the vulnerable.

Secondly, this raises a key point. Whence comes an informed critique of these ideologies that can lay bare their demonic nature and offer alternatives that take seriously both the facts of economic life (which are not always as tractable as we would like them to be) and the facts of the gospel of God? We all share — and by that I mean Christians, socialists, non-monetarist economists both in the third world and in the UK — the obloquy for having failed in that task. Yes, we complained; we protested; we even ridiculed the so-called intellectual basis of Friedmanite monetarism. But we did not adequately or sustainedly subject it to the judgment of God. We behaved as though it were a neutral set of ideas, to be judged on its intellectual merits. We did not see it for what it was: a demonic power that has brought death, disaster, depression and misery to tens of millions of God's poor throughout the world . . . It has passed. But as we survey the future, can we be confident that Christian socialists will confront the next ideology that treats human beings only as variables in a set of equations?

I think we are the more likely to do so if we keep one ear cocked for those of our friends and allies who live and work in countries where many of our own problems and dilemmas are mirrored — and magnified.

This lecture was given in March, 1987.

Tony Benn
The moral basis of the radical left
The best hope for the future of British politics

The legacy of R. H. Tawney

Political argument in Britain today is becoming more fundamental as the old consensus breaks down under the inherent defects of capitalism. This breakdown is, in turn, dissolving the modest welfare society which has been established, and eroding liberalism itself.

Never has democratic socialism been more necessary. But never has its struggle to assert itself been more difficult, first because it is constantly and maliciously misrepresented by a mass media which increasingly acts as a propaganda machine rather than an information service and, secondly, because it suffers from the experience of Labourism under successive Labour governments since the second world war, which often was not socialism, even though it was presented as such both by its advocates and its opponents.

The price we have paid for failing to establish even a base for socialism over the last 30 years is that a renewed and most virulent strain of capitalism is now in the ascendancy. The only 'opposition' being permitted to be heard by the establishment is a weak, centralist, liberalism, on occcasion misappropriating the word 'socialism', behind which authoritarian forces can muster and the trade union movement can be broken.

Resistance to monetarism or the imposition of the old consensus wrapped up in new coalition alignments cannot be entrusted to an oppositon rhetoric which simply heaps abuse upon ministers who are carrying out traditional capitalist remedies. The true nature of this crisis must be understood and explained.

This understanding and this explanation must be widely spread before socialist answers can be evolved as a guide for the future. It is at this very moment that the Labour Party is coming to realise the price it has paid for its long neglect of socialism as a tool of analysis, as a set of moral values and as the inspiration for both political action and political education.

Fortunately, the labour movement has its own tradition of socialist writing upon which it can call, and none greater than came from R. H. Tawney. The papers which he wrote are a part of that inheritance and will give a new generation of socialists an insight into the unique nature of Tawney's mind, morality and motivation.

For some years Tawney has been quoted extensively by right wing members of the Labour Party who have tried to make him appear as the father of their own school of revisionist thought. Yet Tawney spelled out his socialist objectives with great simplicity: 'The fundamental question, as always, is: Who is to be master?

Is the reality behind the decorous drapery of political democracy to continue to be the economic power wielded by a few thousand — or, of that be preferred, a few hundred thousand — bankers, industrialists and landowners?

'Or shall a serious effort be made — as serious, for example, as was made, for other purposes, during the war — to create organs through which the nation can control, in cooperation with other nations, its economic destinies; plan its business as it deems most conducive to the general well being; override, for the sake of economic efficiency, the obstruction of vested interests; and distribute the product of its labours in accordance with some generally recognised priniciples of justice?

'Capitalist parties presumably accept the first alternative. A socialist party chooses the second. The nature of its business is determined by its choice.'

Tawney accepted the 'existence of a class struggle' and argued for the 'transference of economic power to public hands' which, in his view, had to 'take precedence over the mere alleviation of distress'. Thus he placed himself firmly on the side of all those within the Labour party who are now calling for socialism in place of the weak and woolly liberalism which has so deeply penetrated Labour politics during the last 30 years.

One of the most scurrilous charges levelled by the right wing against socialists in the Labour Party is that our policies would endanger political liberty. Tawney meets that charge head on and rebuts it completely: '. . . the suggestion that capitalism, at the present stage of its history, is the guardian of any liberties but its own is an implausible affectation . . . it would more properly be described as the parent of a new feudalism.'

He sees a serious danger that, if the conditions of freedom are too long delayed, 'the failure to achieve it may discredit democracy'.

Tawney places all this argument in its proper moral framework. As a convinced democrat and Christian socialist, he saw Marx as being 'as saturated with ethics as a Hebrew prophet' and argues that 'Christianity and popular communism — though not, it appears, the official variety — are alike in holding the now unfashionable view that principles really matter.'

Christians and socialists versus capitalists and militarists — the politics of the next century

Looking ahead to the politics of the twenty-first century, worldwide, it is now possible to imagine a new line-up of forces between those who follow the ethical values of Christianity and the economic analysis of socialism on the one hand, and the forces of capitalism and militarism on the other. The rich and the powerful will set up hierarchies of authority with leadership coming from the top and the rest will look downwards and outwards to the cellular strength of grass-roots movement that does not seek uniformity of compliance and faith.

To identify the lines of argument between Christian socialism and capitalist militarism may come as a surprise to those who have been persuaded that the real choice lies between a democracy which depends upon capitalism and an atheistic communist dictatorship. Yet any serious and unbiased observer of the world scene today can already observe the outlines of the analysis that I am offering in the actual circumstances of our time.

Recently in South Africa, as militaristic capitalism strengthens its oppression of the disinherited, it is the churches and the labour movement who are coming forward as major defenders of the oppressed. In Latin America it is the liberation theologians who are catholics and Marxists who are uniting against the power of the military dictators defending American and domestic capitalist exploitation.

The present state of British politics

If we are to understand the full significance of this alternative view we need a much more fundamental look at our society than is currently permitted, where the present level of political debate is immensely shallow.

In Britain today we seem to accept a criminal neglect of human need and an unforgivable waste of human skill which flow directly from the grossly unequal distribution of wealth and power and resources.

We are seeing a systematic destruction of democratic institutions, the wholesale control of information, the entrenchment of privilege and a contempt for those who try to introduce ideas that challenge the present hierarchy.

We are seeing the deliberate stimulation of fear, which produces nationalism, suspicion and distrust and is the breeding ground for discrimination against women, blacks, gays and all minorities, particularly those who dissent.

We are taught to worship money and power at the expense of the community. The hours of TV broadcasting time and pages of newspaper coverage dealing with money matters have elevated them into a religion that has obscured and overlaid the moral values taught over the centuries by Christians and socialists who represent traditions of human concern.

In the name of money we are despoiling the environment, exhausting natural resources and exploiting the animal kingdom.

Presiding over all this we have parliamentary arguments and media coverage that are often superficial and shallow and confined to personalities who exchange abuse, armed primarily with slogans drawn from the think tanks of the advertising agencies. Indeed, as the situation gets worse, there are clear signs that the governing classes in all political parties are huddling together nervously, united by a denunciation of all those who question the central tenets of the establishment — identifying them as extremists, loonies, revolutionaries, wreckers or mindless militants who can be lumped together, as 'the enemy within', and are best dealt with by the security services or by the disciplinary machinery of the Labour Party.

And if the dissent expresses itself in demonstrations then the riot police are called in and the ultimate weapon is a shoot-to-kill policy authorised by crown prerogatives and upheld by the courts as necessary in the interest of national security.

But it would be wrong to seek to place the responsibility for all that has happened on the people at the top. For we are all accessories by our acceptance of this system, expressed through the ballot box in elections which make those who vote for the status quo, expressed in any political party, guilty of collusion with what is being done.

If all or most of these charges against the present British political set-up can be sustained — as I believe they can be — it must be obvious that any serious attempt to improve our society will call for a strategy of reform that goes far beyond anything that has been discussed, agreed or attempted by any major political party in Britain.

Policies may change with differing circumstances and, unless we have a clear idea of the criteria which should guide policy, we can sink into a swamp of pragmatism or ad hockery. Here everything that has to be done is looked at in isolation, without any regard to what came before or what will follow or to parallel issues that bear upon the decisions that need to be made.

Reviving the democratic challenge

The time has come when we should all be asking who has the power, how did they get it, in whose interests do they use it, to whom are they accountable and how can they be removed? These are really fundamental questions and, when they are asked and answers are insisted upon, the rich and the strong begin to tremble and hit back with all the force at their command because they know they have been rumbled and their power is being challenged.

Considering the fact that Britain prides itself on having the mother of parliaments which, it is told, is the envy of the world, it is amazing how little discussion there is about how we are actually governed. For, unlike even the Americans, who elect their president, their Senate, their House of Representatives, their state governors and assemblies and some judges and magistrates, Britain has a hereditary monarch and a House of Lords based on heredity and patronage. The House of Commons is cramped and confined virtually to an observer role by the fact that all the powers of a mediaeval monarch have been preserved for exercise by a prime minister who is an elected dictator and has become the real fount of honour and patronage which corrupts the democratic process.

In truth Britain is still a very primitive society and is class-ridden from top to bottom. The institution of monarchy lends legitimacy to a mass of mediaeval class distinctions that we have never been able to eliminate from our system. Even the leaders of the labour movement expect on retirement to receive peerages and knighthoods and, when thus co-opted, they serve to prop up the very structures which they are initially elected to dismantle.

For it must be obvious to any serious socialist that you cannot create a new society by trying to use the institutions established by another class for another purpose in another period of history. One of the great defects of the labour movement is that it has devoted so little attention to institutional and constitutional questions, tamely assuming that an incoming Labour government can take charge at once and that, the state being neutral, its structures can be used to serve us.

Yet all the evidence suggests that there is now immense public interest in and support for major reforms in the structure of the state.

The importance of moral values

The rock upon which any society must be built is its conception of moral values. This reveals how it sees the relationship between human beings one to another here and worldwide. Do we see our life as being forever condemned to be of cut-throat competition in a jungle where the strongest run off with all the prizes and the weakest go to the wall? Or, by contrast, do we perceive the human race as linked in brotherhood and sisterhood with common interests requiring policies that advance those interests?

These are absolutely basic questions and, until we resolve them in our own minds, we cannot make head or tail of the political matters which come up for decision nor can we even argue the case for democracy which is based on the equal rights of people to share in the government of their country.

It is a fact that in Britain today and in most of the capitalist world, we are being taught to elevate profit above need, to worship power and neglect distress and to obey orders from the top. These are the guiding principles of our society and, if we do not challenge them head on, we may succeed in changing the management of the status quo, amending the policies which the management follows, and doing some good thereby, but we shall never, ever get to the root of what is wrong.

The roots of socialism

The roots of socialism go back deep into our history, long before the word was used or its modern meaning was attached. Demands for justice and peace and equality have always been implanted in the human soul and have been pressed upon tyrants over the centuries. Trade unionism, drawing its strength from collective action, was developed to provide a route by which these demands could be achieved collectively. Robert Owen, the first socialist, played a significant part in developing the cooperative movement and Charles Kingsley brought his Christian conscience to bear on the injustices of Victorian society.

But, of course, it was Karl Marx in *Das Kapital* who turned his formidable intellect to a study of the nature of capitalism. He analysed with crystal clarity the inherent conflict of interest between those who create the wealth by their labour and those who own it and control it. This class analysis has persisted because it is so self-evidently true. Without the bag of tools that Marx bequeathed to us, we cannot understand the world in which we live, even today when capitalism has changed so much in the century that has passed since Marx's death.

Yet the idea of class struggle and the consequences that flow from those conceptions have not only terrified the establishment but also brought many good Christians to a parting of the ways with socialism. They see the ideas of class conflict as running counter to the ideas of human brotherhood which should bring boss and worker, landlord and serf, king and subject into a relationship of cooperation that melts away all differences.

Class: Christians and the new realism

This Christian revulsion against the idea of class conflict has now been reinforced by the new realists in the labour movement. They have suddenly come up with the novel idea that the working class has disappeared and that the main function of trade unions is to enter into cosy agreements with the employers that will increase productivity and competitiveness and thus make Britain a more successful capitalist country.

I must confess that I find neither of these arguments very persuasive, for Christians who reject class struggle sometimes forget that Marx looked forward to a classless society. And those who believe that modern technology has abolished class as a factor in modern politics have got to explain the widening gap betwen rich and poor, here and worldwide, fuelled by greater and greater degrees of exploitation which have been concealed behind bigger and bigger propaganda budgets.

Much as I admire the motivation of those who have worked for famine relief in the third world, I do not believe that a modern, international version of the old Victorian Lady Bountiful can be any sort of a substitute for a clinical critique of the mechanisms by which the poor are harnessed like horses to pull the carriages of the rich.

It is true that the ideas of socialism when they were put into practice fell far short of what their founders had hoped. To give reality to Christian ethics and socialist humanism, the advocates of both may have to find themselves drawn together out of the structures of the organised churches and the organised parties. They would then have to try to inject the essential message which brings them together back into those organisations which should be preaching it, in order to revive the essential teachings upon which each were founded.

Towards a policy for peace

One area of policy where this is being attempted and must be done is the field of foreign and defence policy. Any objective observer of the condition of humanity now could not fail to be astonished by the enormous expenditure on weapons of war in every country in the world, gobbling up money, human skill and technical resources at a time when millions starve for lack of a dirt road, a clean water supply, a tractor or a simple clinic.

Yet we are slowly coming to realise that our own security forces, which are now one of the most powerful political institutions in Britain, taxing us heavily, computerising their dossiers on us and always standing ready to take power if the status quo were really challenged, are actually taking control of us in the guise of protecting our liberties. Christian socialists should challenge the consensus, in favour of high military spending with NATO, in favour of non-alignment and a massive shift of resources from weapons to development.

Useful work for all

Similarly Christian socialists cannot possibly accept the new pessimism which tells us that we can never have full employment again and that the best we can do is to be kind to the unemployed and, if they refuse to work at starvation wages, to conscript them into workfare schemes with incomes just above benefit levels to do the dirty work for the well-to-do and be grateful for the chance of doing so.

If we were now to look at the needs of our society for the young and the old, for women and children, for the sick and the disabled, for homes and schools and clinics and creches and wheelchairs and telephones, and finance them by public expenditure on the scale of our wartime budgets, everyone would be back at work and our economy would be booming as the engine of recovery was set into motion again by the injection of public expenditure.

But why then is it not done? The answer is simple. There is no profit to be made from meeting needs that are not backed by money which the poor do not have. Capitalism cannot adjust itself to do what has to be done. We had better be honest about this and not pretend that a new hand on the tiller will steer the capitalist ship into calmer waters on the turbulent sea of market forces.

If technology does allow us to provide what we need with less back-breaking effort, then let us go for retirement at 55, a 35-hour week, and raise the school leaving age to 90. The task of socialist economic policy is not to find new ways of manipulating forces that are inimical to our human interests but to replace those forces by others that have been devised to meet those interests.

Christian socialists will have to think about these things too. For not only does the worship of money corrupt our morality but also it has now degenerated into a form of witchcraft. The high priests of the City tell us, with straight faces, on an hourly basis, what has happened to the Dow Jones Industrial Index and the pound sterling to three points of decimals compared to a basket of European currencies and persuade us that, as a result, we had better close some more hospitals and cut the dole.

Fellowship, collectivism and freedom

One other priority to which Christian socialists should address themselves is how to unite the ideas associated with fellowship and collective effort with freedom, to make it real in a pluralistic society where equality does not mean uniformity or meritocracy but makes it possible for us to be ourselves within the human family. Such a task would take us far beyond the relatively simple question of repealing the repressive laws that have been passed to restirct trade unions, local authorities, women, the black community, gays and dissenters. We have to re-establish the rights of freedom of thought, freedom of speech, the right to be heard and the right to be different, partly in our statutes but more fundamentally in our minds.

To be candid, the idea of freedom of this kind has been unwelcome to many who call themselves Christians or socialists, at various periods in our history, and it will always be a struggle to reassert it whoever is in power.

It is easy to be pessimistic in the period of history in which we live but pessimism paralyses the will and creates that solid pedestal of compliance which the establishment needs to preserve its power. If we allow that pessimism to grip us we shall be guilty of sustaining the very system which must be changed.

It would be wrong to try to appropriate the name of Tawney to justify all the arguments I have advanced, but my understanding of his teachings certainly gave me the hope to believe that social justice is possible and certainly has given hope to many others too.

This lecture was given in March, 1988.

Pauline Webb

The media and social morality

It comes as both an honour and a relief to be invited to speak on an occasion such as this. The honour comes in recalling the person in whose memory this lecture is endowed, and in noting the distinguished list of my predecessors as lecturers, not many I notice of my gender, but at least all of them expressing a socialist commitment (and therefore, I dare to hope, a feminist commitment) that I share. And that is what brings a sense of relief too. At least on this occasion I can make quite clear the standpoint from which I speak. I am so accustomed to being professionally obliged to sit on a fence in a BBC studio or to avoid giving offence in a Methodist pulpit that I welcome the chance here to stand personally with both feet firmly on socialist ground, confident that I speak to those who share the same basic premise that underlies the substance of what I want to say today.

I speak as one who, contrary to some current political opinion, does believe in such a concept as 'society' which binds us all together, whether we perceive ourselves particularly as individuals or members of families or national citizens. We are primarily members of one human society, caught up in a global, interdependent and mutually responsible network of relationships. As a committed socialist, I believe that within such a society the resources vital to the welfare of all should be publicly owned, that those managing such resources should be openly accountable and that the resources themselves should be used in such a way as to enrich the life of every part of the community. And as a Christian I believe one of the most valuable of all human resources is the ability to communicate, communication itself being that which, by definition, binds us together in one. We communicate when we share a message with one another, we communicate when we open a door between two separate corridors (especially corridors of power) and we communicate when we meet with God and with one another at the Lord's table.

Central to our faith is a God who communicates with us through the media of word and scarament. And both those media are not static but dynamic. The word of God speaks through events. It is always a happening. 'Dabar' said the Hebrew prophets. 'The word of God *happened* to us' and their prophetic role consisted of reporting, interpreting and commenting upon those events. It was a true and lively word, and many are the warnings against those who treat words falsely or lightly. Likewise the sacrament, in which eternal truths are made visible for us, carries with it a kind of health warning against the making of false images or believing that the image is more important than the reality. And the ultimate medium, or rather mediator, becomes the word made flesh and dwelling among us.

I begin on that theological note because I think it helps to put everything I want to say about the media into perspective. The media are never ends in themselves. They are always only means to an end, and must be judged by the ends that they

110

serve. For the purposes of this lecture, by 'media' I mean particularly those electronic, mass media of communication which are now capable of encircling the globe and even beam down upon us from extra-terrestrial heights. I am fully aware that these are not the only media of communication. It was refreshing when I was in Kenya recently, for a conference on women in media, to meet African women who still stressed the importance of such traditional media as folk-drama, talking drums and even textile patterns. But they too acknowledged the pervasiveness and greater persuasive power of the so-called mass media of radio and television.

I say 'so-called' because these are not strictly speaking 'mass' media at all. Though they number their audiences in millions, they do in effect address them in ones and twos, and in that sense are among the most intimate, and indeed insidious, of all forms of communication. I am aware too of the power of that veteran among the mass media, the printed word, but in this lecture I want to concentrate attention on what is happening in the world I know best, the world of television and radio, rather than in the press, in the strict sense of that term. In many ways the concerns about all these areas coincide, since many of these means of communication are now in the possession of the same mogul empires.

My concern with 'morality' in this lecture is not so much focussed on those codes of personal conduct which provoke a chorus of disapproval of such evils as screen violence, bad language and explicit sex (either before or after 9pm!), much as all of these are to be deplored, but rather on the ends that these media serve within society as a whole. For whom do they mediate, what is the message they carry, how do they serve to enrich or to impoverish the lives of those they affect?

One word of warning before I embark on the subject proper. What I have to say will inevitably be of a tentative and ephemeral nature, for so rapidly is the whole media landscape changing around us that what we say one week can be outdated the next. Trying to prepare this lecture has been rather like trying to build a house while such a hurricane is howling around that you cannot keep the roof on. In the media business you can say quite literally now that not even the Sky is the limit!

But first, as they say when they outline the menu of a radio magazine, first let us look back at the beginning of it all, that stable past when things stood still long enough for some kind of guidelines to be laid down. What end did the pioneers of radio and television intend these new media to serve? It is astonishing to realise that the whole enterprise is less than 100 years old, and that this century has seen greater developments in the means of human communication than all the past 1900 years, even allowing for that one great quantum leap brought about by the invention of printing. The first ever radio broadcast was made to ships at sea by a Canadian experimenter, in code and voice radio, on Christmas eve 1906. His message consisted of a passage from St Luke's gospel, a violin solo of Gounod's *O Holy Night* and a woman singing Handel's *Largo* — a programme that extended, as it were, the outreach of the angels' Christmas message, 'Peace on earth to those of good will'.

Such is the nature of the machinations of the human mind, however, that the military possibilities of this new medium were rapidly recognised and the first pratical uses of wireless telegraphy were by the army during the first world war. Even then, however, an American engineer called David Sarnoff prophesied that he could foresee the day when radio would become a household utility rather like a piano, so that everyone could enjoy music in their own home.

Very soon it was realised that this new experimental toy could rapidly get out of hand and, as wireless manufacturers saw the possibilities of new mass markets for their wares, governments began to recognise, too, the need to control the competition for the air-waves and limit the number of transmitting stations. Here in Britain the result was the forming of the British Broadcasting Company, under the directorship of that dour Scottish Calvinist, John Reith. who saw this responsibility as a divinely ordained vocation. He rapidly turned the company into an independent corporation, under royal charter and financed by a licence fee agreed by the British government. Resolutely resisting any kind of commercial or political control, Reith turned what had begun as a business arrangement into a moral crusade. Even the name of this new activity, broadcasting, was taken from the agricultural metaphor of the New Testament parable, a fact enshrined in the statue of the sower which still stands in the entrance hall of Broadcasting House. Moreover, Reith ordered that, written indelibly in letters of gold over the portals of that new headquarters, should be the clear aim of broadcasting as he saw it. 'This temple of the muses,' reads the Latin quotation, still resplendent there today, 'is dedicated to almighty God by the first governors of broadcasting, Sir John Reith being governor general. It is their prayer that good seeds sown may bring forth a good harvest, that all things hostile to peace and purity may be banished from this house, that the people, inclining their ears to whatsoever things are beautiful, honest and of good report, may tread the paths of wisdom and righteousness.'

Thus it was, on such firm moral foundation, that one of the first broadcasting networks in the world was established more than 60 years ago. Meanwhile, on the other side of the Atlantic where, as one American put it, 'we never had a Lord Reith and, if we had, we wouldn't have known what to do with him,' radio stations were proliferating without any controls. By 1926 president Hoover described it as '10,000 telephone subscribers crying through the air for their mates,' and warned that, 'soon the ether will be filled with frantic chaos.' Here too it became obvious that there had to be some management of the air waves. A system of franchises for radio stations evolved, financed mainly by air time being bought by commercial sponsors.

Very soon after this, shadowy images were beginning to appear on the screen that heralded the coming of television. By 1931 the first full-length book on this new medium appeared in which the author, Edgar Felix, predicted that television would have to become a medium financed mainly by advertising. Four years later an exile from Hitler's Germany, Rudolf Arnheim, took that prophecy further. He warned that when television became universally available it would be the most powerful of all the mass media because it would turn into a spectator sport and lead to a cult of sensory stimulation for its own sake. Few people heeded his Cassandra-like warnings or gave any serious consideration as to how this new medium would be managed or controlled.

By then, radio was thriving in the laissez-faire market of American commercialism, on one side of the Atlantic, and the public service tradition firmly established here in Britain. The BBC was still under the stern tutelage of Lord Reith who seems never to have doubted that he knew what was best for people, 'few of whom', he once commented, 'know what they want and fewer of whom know what they need'. He believed that what they needed was information, education and entertainment 'of the purest kind'. He spoke in utopian terms of how these must be made available to the whole population, irrespective of class or background, so that the great and the good of the land might communicate with the humblest and the most degenerate. All this he saw as contributing to the building of a new and more egalitarian society in which all would have the opportunity of education, entertainment and enlightenment.

All that sounds now far away and long go. George Orwell, who worked for the BBC in those days, described it as being like working in a cross between a girls' school and a lunatic asylum. If he were alive today he might feel compelled to use another simile, for it is fast becoming more like working in a market. The nightmare Orwell had, of a 1980s world controlled by media owned and operated by a communist state, is rapidly being replaced by an opposite nightmare, a world controlled by media owned and operated by the market forces of international capitalism. Information, education and entertainment have all become marketable resources and, in common with many other socially beneficial resources in contemporary society, are up for offers to the highest bidders. The whole communications industry is the most rapidly growing industry of our time, employing already some 60 million people across the world. Within the next five years it is likely that 60 per cent of the working population here in Britain will be employed at one level or another in it — in research and development of new technologies; in the manufacture and marketing of hardware; in the creation and management of regional, national and international networks; in the production and selling of programmes and in the ever increasing business of advertising.

And while the west concentrates on developing more and more efficient forms of high technology, worldwide trade in telecommunications is fast becoming a bonanza. The major markets are expected to move, within the next five years, to the third world, where countries like Chile and Morocco head the list of expected increases amounting to more than 100 per cent in their expenditure. Production also is making its inroads into developing nations, as the electronics industry looks for its labour force to third world women, whose delicate fingers will work for long hours and low wages, thus substantially reducing the costs of equipment for which there is such a rapidly escalating and widespread demand. The telecommunications industry, like all the huge multinationals, transcends national boundaries and seeks to set up a worldwide network of communication, like a vast nervous system linking together what Marshall McLuhan described as the 'global village' but which, more appropriately in recent years, has been called the 'global market'.

The more extensive the industry becomes in its outreach, the more intensive is its ownership. Between 10 and 15 percent of the world's largest corporations have considerable stakes in the communications trade as well as in a whole cluster of associated industries. One of the largest of the electronics companies, with outlets in almost every country in the world, is RCA, the major manufacturer of TV sets, VCRs and studio equipment. The same company controls Telex traffic; is a main shareholder in worldwide satellite systems; owns one of America's major educational publishing houses; runs NBC, the main broadcasting network in the USA; has its own recording company and even owns Hertz, the worldwide hire-car firm. With its tentacles thus reaching into every possible area of the communiucations business, this great octopus has good reason to embrace every opportunity to grab by the ears and the eyes the millions of potential listeners and viewers out there, in the unfished ocean, without being too fastidious about the quality of the bait it employs.

The question to be asked is not about the integrity of the programmes themselves, but about how well they hold the interest of the customer-cum-consumer they are being provided for. Audience surveys in the US have been known actually to monitor sweating palms on the viewers of a TV film to assess whether the tension will keep them rivetted to their seats long enough to see the commercial break. And even NBC, the leading and prestigious American broadcasting company, has reduced its news coverage because, as the vice president of programming, Aaron Cohen, put it in a video film on the reality of the media: 'We don't find news to be profitable, so we don't overload with news.'

Now it could be argued by the advocates of free enterprise that a free market opens the air waves to any number of entrepreneurs. All you need, to start your own local radio station, run a national network or even launch a satellite, is the wherewithal to buy the franchise and purchase the equipment. You would need about two million pounds to set up a modest local radio station, 15 million to develop a cable TV network and somewhere in the region of 300 to 400 million to launch a satellite – which does somewhat restrict the number of people able to make such bids! Nevertheless, there are now 2,500 communication satellites in place and another 400 in the pipeline.

They have three different functions. There are those that are used for suveillance and are of such probing accuracy that from the height of 24,000 miles they could read the numberplate on your car. Apart from the new kind of espionage this makes possible, it also gives, to those with access to such monitoring information, power to take appropriate and profitable action. For instance, if a blight is observed on the leaves of a coffee plantation in Brazil, it becomes possible to predict a future shortage of crop and to fix the market accordingly. Then there are satellites used for point-to-point communications which, as they increase their capacity, decrease their costs, and so attract more and more users and greater and greater profit. Then there are the satellites that carry the television channels, the latest of which is the Sky channel owned by Rupert Murdoch who, as someone on radio recently commented, now owns the Sky, the Sun, the Times and Today, which indicates what you might well describe as a cosmic influence! Then in September of this year, using a different kind of receiving equipment which will add yet more cost to the would-be viewer, and more profit to the suppliers of the hardware, British Satellite Broadcasting will be launching three more satellite stations. They will be able to receive and transmit clearer pictures of better quality of definition across the world. They will also make use of the much smaller, dinner-plate size receiving aerials which are now becoming available and which can fit conveniently on to a wall.

If all this were to result in more choice of better programmes shared internationally one could not but welcome the developments. Remembering yet another of Lord Reith's dicta, the one that has become the motto of the BBC, theoretically it would seem that it now does become possible for 'nation to speak peace unto nation'. But present experience of the quality of programmes carried on satellite channels does not give much cause for optimism. For here too market forces have to operate: not only do the suppliers of television channels have to provide programmes that will hold audiences large enough and long enough to satisfy advertisers, but also they need to do this at the minimum possible cost. It can cost anything up to half a million pounds an hour to produce an original, prime-time drama programme and even an hour of fairly straightforward documentary can cost £25,000. On the other hand, an hour of soap opera, produced and packaged elsewhere, can be bought for around £2500, so it is hardly surprising that an audience of something like 350 million people in 85 countries regularly watch *Dallas*. The export of American produced TV programmes, which with such huge domestic markets have probably already covered their costs, is now estimated at around 200,000 hours a year, again producing more consumer audiences.

In Europe, we have heard only this week of steps being taken to provide safeguards against this wholesale incursion of the cheapest forms of American programming into the available TV channels. It appears that a kind of quota system will be introduced restricting the number of foreign origin programmes that can be shown on any one channel. Here in Britain, we are promised that one of the criteria to be considered in the granting of franchises will be the proven quality of the kind of programmes to be included in the output. But there is no doubt that there is bound to be a marked shift in emphasis from the kind of creativity which produces programmes that simply have intrinsic, artistic merit to the much more pragmatic approach of providing programmes that are cheap to make or buy or that can attract enough advertising to earn their keep. A bold experiment in television drama such as *The Singing Detective*, or even the more innovative recent series of *Talking Heads*, will be at risk. Either they will have to find sponsors prepared to risk their patronage or they will be confined to some kind of subscription service, which seems to be what is envisaged as the continuing form of public service broadcasting. Like so many other institutions that began originally as a 'public' service – public schools, for example – the BBC could be in danger of ending up as an elitist service available only to those who can afford to buy it.

But if the European countries feel concerned about the likely impact of the global television market, one can imagine how third world countries feel in face of this newest onslaught from the west. At the conference on women in media which I attended recently in Kenya, women engaged in media in one way or another in 10 different African countries came together to discuss these very issues. There were some positive things to be said. Radio and television could be of great service in developing countries, if they could be used to enhance the quality of people's lives and to enlarge their experience. We were given examples of the ways in which radio programmes, video shows and local television stations were playing a role in education for development, in preserving cultural traditions, even by-passing the need for literacy campaigns in giving instruction in matters like agriculture, health care and nutrition. But none of these home-made products can hope to compete in attractiveness with the American based movies and alluring advertisements. Thus the poor are constantly subjected to pressures to buy things which will make them poorer still.

One group at the conference portrayed the dilemma vividly in a play they performed as part of their workshop on drama as a medium of communication. The scene was outside a village home where a woman was milking her cow, with a transistor radio playing in the background. The radio was playing that catchy song, well-suited you might think to this new international network of communication, *I'd like to teach the world to sing in perfect harmony*. The song is, of course, the song of the Coca-Cola company and was followed by enticing descriptions of how all the world's children loved Coca-Cola. Meanwhile, the woman is visited by the owner of a tourist hotel who persuades her to sell the milk so that she then has the money to go and buy coke. Her children love the coke but their bodies need the milk. It takes a lot of persuasion on the part of a health worker before she refuses to sell her milk, resists the temptation to buy the coke and gives her children the milk to drink. There were great cheers when, as the curtain line of the play, she went to the radio, snapped it off and said, 'That's nonsense!' Her media awareness had been born as she learned how to resist what has been called the new 'colonisation' of the world.

Thus do the transnationals exploit this glorious new opportunity for global communication to make it serve their own economic interests. They turn the whole world into one great market, tempting us all to buy things we did not know we needed until the advertisers persuaded us we did. The envy and greed thus inculcated are sins quite as deadly as the lust and violence for which the media are so often condemned, and are equally dangerous to society's health.

But not everyone who seeks to control the media is in it solely for the money. Even that cosmic media man to whom I have already referred, Rupert Murdoch — who owns 70 per cent of the printed press in his own country Australia (he is prevented by law there from taking over television ownership as well), more newspapers in this country than anyone else as well as four of the largest TV networks in the USA — appears to have ambitions that go beyond mere mercenary motives. A recent radio profile of him put it: 'He never walks away with just money. He also walks away with power.' And the power he seems to relish most is the power over that most valuable of all human assets, information. The right to freedom of information is one of the most cherished of all human freedoms. Milton defined it as, 'the liberty to know, to utter and to argue freely according to conscience'. So whoever controls the flow of information usurps a power that properly belongs to the people and introduces a rogue element into the workings of democracy.

This brings us into the whole political dimension of our discussion of the media and morality, and again a glance back into history may help us to see, in clearer perspective, what is happening in the media world today. It is fascinating to note how every major development in the media of communication has been associated with some radical change in society. The invention of the printing press led not only to the possibility (greatly feared by the church) of putting the Bible into the hands of the people, but also played a vital role in the Reformation and the challenge to the political power of the Pope. The French revolution owed much to the advent of the magazine as a way of disseminating information among the people, just as the Russian revolution coincided with the growth in newspaper publishing. And I am old enough myself to remember the way in which radio (or 'the wireless' as we called it then) came into its own during the second world war. From being the guardian of public morals that Lord Reith had envisaged, it became the great upholder of society's morale and the voice of free Europe to the beleagured nations on the continent. The most important programme became the news and the second most important programme the light entertainment shows which made the people laugh and the enemy look ridiculous. The BBC came to be trusted as the source of reliable information in a world of rumour and of wholesome entertainment in a world of terror. 'In a world of poison,' said Leon Blum, the French socialist leader, 'the BBC became the great antiseptic.'

The other side of this coin, however, is that the power of mass communication had also been demonstrated in the rise of fascism in Germany, where one of the most indelible images of the 1930s is of the mass rallies addressed by the frenzied oratory of Adolf Hitler. 'Propaganda, propaganda, propaganda,' said Hitler after the unsuccessful putsch in 1923. 'All that matters is propaganda,' and he became fascinated by the new technologies of mass communication at that time emerging in the USA and Britain. Broadcasting was seen as a crucial weapon of warfare. 'The purpose of news broadcasting,' said Goebbels, 'is to wage war, not to give out information.'

The role of the mass media in enabling Hitler to capture power in Germany drew the attention of a group of German intellectuals — the 'Frankfurt school' of writers — who became refugees from Nazi Germany, having seen their books burned but radio sets proliferating under Hitler's regime. By the time they had settled in the USA, television also was coming into its own. The Frankfurt writers came to believe that these media, by their very nature, would make a population vulnerable to fascist domination. Individual creativity would be crushed by the impact of mass entertainment. And people would be discouraged from taking any personal part in the political process because politics would be turned into a spectator sport. In his book, *The Eclipse of Reason*, Horkheimer wrote in 1947: 'As ordinary people withdraw from participating in political affairs, society tends to revert to the law of the jungle, which crushes all vestiges of individuality.' The sociologist T. W. Adorno argued: 'The mass media can create an aura which makes the spectator seem to experience a non-existent actuality.'

Having spent the last four months of 1988 in Canada, where I watched both the American and Canadian elections, I can vouch for the accuracy of the prediction that TV would turn politics into a spectator sport: the issues to be raised, the context in which political discussion was set, the personality profiles of the leaders to be elected, were all dependent upon the whim and the wit of television producers and presenters. And we have of course seen the same thing happening in the political process in Britain, where the political agenda can be set by the attention the media give, or do not give, to the issues at stake.

One striking, early example of this was the election speech given in the 1960s by a comparatively unknown politician in a small church hall. It was picked up by the media and heard or read by 86 per cent of the population two days later. From then on, Enoch Powell and his dire warnings about immigration had become headline news which affected the whole country's views of the race issue. In a Gallup poll shortly before the speech, only 6 per cent thought immigration an issue of national importance. After the speech, 27 per cent thought it important and nearly 70 per cent of the public thought the government should take 'a harder line'. Racism had been brought on to the national agenda.

At this point it is worth emphasising that in this country we have become accustomed to a certain liberal tradition governing the kind of views that can be expressed within the media. The BBC and, following the same tradition, the IBA, have always claimed to be objective and balanced in their presentation of news and current affairs comment. Mind you, one can argue whether complete objectivity is ever possible. I am reminded of the story of the slightly senile judge who, in his summing up, advised the jury that they should strive to be 'neither partial nor impartial'. Total impartiality is impossible to achieve. I also like the story of the news editor who, exasperated by accusations of lack of balance in his presentation of news, phoned the religious department and said, 'There's a guy here who says you haven't represented his case fairly. His name is Pontius Pilate'. Clearly there are limitations on what kind of views ought to be expressed on a medium that claims to uphold the values of a civilised society.

But of course the vital question is the one that Pilate himself posed: 'What is truth?' And who decides what information is to be shared? I want to come to the defence of many journalists I know who do in fact relentlessly seek to ferret out the truth, even to the embarrassment of people who would have preferred to keep their dishonesties hidden. The stereotype of key-hole peeping hacks invading people's privacy is not, I believe, worthy of the profession as a whole. There are such people as honest reporters, there are fair-minded editors, there are even truthful managers of news agencies. And we can all recall events of recent political history which have been profoundly affected by the relentless pursuit of truth by journalists. They have been endowed with that nose of curiosity and those antennae which tingle at deception that are essential faculties in our profession.

Good journalists are, as it were, the eyes and ears of the public, bringing to light the deeds of those who, as scripture reminds us, might well prefer the dark because their deeds are evil. Not surprisingly, therefore, journalists are not the most popular people with those who hold the reins of power, because one of the great tools of power is the possession of information. Those in power like to keep their secrets. But as Lord Acton said: 'Everything secret degenerates; nothing is safe that does not show how it can bear discussion and publicity.' And, as Colin Morris once put it: 'Governments hoard secrets like squirrels hoard nuts, far more than they ever require.'

So who decide what information becomes public and where is that information gathered from? The first thing one realises when one works in the media is that there is no shortage of news. It pours into news rooms at the rate of 150 words a minute all hours of the day. Most of it originates from four major press agencies, all of them in the western part of the world. There are also monitoring services keeping an ear and an eye on what is being reported in other parts of the world. In the case of large corporations, such as the BBC, there are also specialist correspondents and reporters stationed in crucial places all over the globe. So much news is coming in that only 1 per cent of the available information is actually used. The other 99 per cent is discarded. That means that someone has to make selective decisions as to what is newsworthy. There are certain thumbnail criteria commonly accepted in journalism: is it recent? is it reliable? is it related to other stories? does it have any local significance for the audience? is it happening to someone already in the public eye and so on. But the advent of television has added another, searching question: are there pictures to go with the story? This has led to the development of a market in news film, where every day available film emanating from an agency such as Visnews, sited in London but with cameras at the ready in all parts of the world, are put on offer. If at least three of the 90 different countries subscribing to the service show an interest in a particular material then it can be made immediately available — but all at a price of course. So the wealthiest parts of the world become the most important customers and their choices tend to determine what everyone else sees. The poorer countries have to depend on what others choose to let them know, even sometimes about their own areas of the world. Thus what Peru learns about Columbia may well depend upon a story and pictures coming through London.

There is no such thing as a free flow of information. But it is important to note that the first casualty in any struggle for political power is the editorial control of the media. That is why journalists of integrity, and let me repeat that I still believe there are many such, set their faces steadfastly against any attempts to have that control wrested from them, whether the pretext for such interference be on grounds of national security, state secrecy or political expediency. The processing, packaging and marketing of news is a precious privilege, to be safeguarded for the welfare of the whole of society to whom that information rightly belongs.

Yet we live in a time of quite unprecedented interference in media affairs by all kinds of vested interests. Recent legislation here in Britain about who may or may not be interviewed, for example, in northern Ireland, introduces a measure of government editorial control never before experienced in the public broadcasting service. Political attacks on the integrity of journalists making programmes like the recent ITV documentary, *Death on the Rock*, or like that on one of the BBC's most distinguished reporters, Kate Adie, in Libya, are disturbing trends. And even the justified outcry about the erosion of standards of personal morality in much that passes for popular entertainment threatens to lead to measures of pre-censorship of a severity comparable only to Oliver Cromwell's draconian measures against the press. For the question to be asked about any kind of censorship is: 'Who is censoring whom and whose interests are they serving?' It has been said that censorship is almost always political, rather than moral, in that it serves the interests of people in power.

I liked the comment of David Bridge in an address on the future of broadcasting to a recent president's council of the Methodist church: 'The choice is not between regulation and de-regulation but between the right kind and the wrong kind of regulation . . . The wrong kind could place enormous power in very few hands, with the result that the freedom of broadcasters will come to mean the freedom to broadcast as many of Rupert Murdoch's prejudices as William Rees Mogg (editor of *The Times*) judges will not offend our wives or servants or startle the horses.'

There are some people who wonder whether claims are not grossly exaggerated that television viewing radically influences behaviour or changes opinion. The results of recent surveys have been ambivalent in their evidence. But it is certain that advertisers and politicians are convinced that it does. Otherwise they would not spend so much of their energy and expenditure on packaging their wares for the viewers.

What does this say to those of us who, from a religious view point, believe that we also have a message to proclaim and that both word and image are God-given and God-chosen media of communication? I do not believe that it means we too have to get into the market and open our own TV religious broadcasting channel. Attempts I have seen on the other side of the Atlantic have seemed to me to result either in a terrible distortion of the gospel, to make it fit into the success-orientated materialism of so much TV programming, or in extravagant attempts to present an ideal portrait of the church which bears little resemblance to its human reality. Religious broadcasting needs to go much deeper than that, in remaining an integral part of the network; in questioning the very values implicit in the medium it serves; in warning against the dangers of deceiving words and false images; and in being prepared to fulfil the humble and precarious role of the mere sower of seeds that may help still, in all the threatening jungle of the media, to bring forth a good harvest for the welfare of all the people.

In conclusion may I suggest three actions we could take:

1 In responding to the government's white paper on broadcasting, we should make it clear that we believe that broadcasting is too valuable a human resource to be bought and sold in the market place. It should be used so as to make available to all people, irrespective of what they earn or where they live, the opportunity of receiving reliable information, continuing education and wholesome entertainment. We should also stress the need for the BBC to continue to receive sufficient resources through the licensing fee to continue providing a wide ranging public service to the whole community.

2 We should encourage young people of integrity and commitment to ideals of social justice to go into the profession of journalism, recognising it to be an honoured profession and one in which it is possible to exercise a Christian vocation, in either the secular or the religious spheres.

3 We should ourselves keep a critical watch on the media and encourage media awareness training within the communities we can influence, refusing to become involved in a mere spectator sport and actively exercising our personal and political responsibility to ensure that these powerful media really do become, in a free society, the purveyors of the good, the beautiful and the true. As Wendell Phillips put it: 'Eternal vigilance is the price of our liberty.'

This lecture was given in March, 1989.

Peter Dawe
Epilogue
The Christian Socialist Movement

The Christian Socialist Movement, which celebrated its thirtieth anniversary as the 1990's opened, holds a unique position in British political and religious life. As heir to a long tradition of radical Christian social thought, it brings together Christians of all denominations and various theologies who share a common belief that democratic socialism is the practical, political expression of their faith.

The inaugural meeting on January 22, 1960, in the Kingsway Hall, London, resulted from the amalgamation of the Society of Socialist Clergy and Ministers with the Socialist Christian League. The formation of the movement followed the issuing of a manifesto, *Papers from the lamb*, on May Day 1959 — its title owing less to the Book of Revelation than to the Holborn pub of its origin — and signed by among others Tom Driberg, John Groser, Donald Soper and Mervyn Stockwood. R. H. Tawney made one of this last public appearances at the movement's first meeting.

Donald Soper chaired the movement until becoming its president in 1975 and was ably succeeded by Canon Edward Charles who led the new drive for membership which was launched in 1977. Highpoints of that period where the well attended public meetings forcefully addressed by the late Bishop Colin Winter of Namibia and the relaunch of the quarterly *Christian Socialist* magazine in a modern format in 1982. In 1983 Canon Charles became a vice president of the movement.

The movement has always sought to relate to both the churches and the Labour movement. Public meetings have invariably been held at both Labour Party and Methodist conferences. The CSM banner has been present at trade union rallies including Tolpuddle, peace marches and various demonstrations in London.

The Christian socialist case is presented in the annual Tawney lectures in London and by a series of residential conferences starting at the University of Kent at Canterbury in 1982 and followed by Hengrave Hall, Suffolk; Cliff College, Derbyshire; Luton Industrial College; Scargill House, Yorkshire and the Pilgrims Centre, Walsingham. At these conferences, where themes have ranged from Christian-Marxist dialogue to environmental issues, the movement seeks whenever possible to give a platform to women and black Christian socialists. A similar aim exists for public meetings.

The movement realises that its influence is best served by cooperating with sympathetic groups. In the 1980s it was a leading member of the radical Christian coalition, Christian Organisations for Social, Political and Economic Change, and also affiliated to the International League of Religious Socialists.

A major development in extending the movement's political influence was its affiliation to the Labour Party in 1988, as one of the socialist societies, the first organisation to be accepted for several years. Some CSM branches are also affiliated to their local constituency parties.

The Christian Socialist Movement now has a membership of more than 1,200 people who include more than 20 Labour MPs, an MEP, a trade union general secretary, the former general secretary of the Trades Union Congress, councillors, clergy and members of all denominations. A growing number of local and regional branches organise day conferences with leading Christian socialist speakers.

We invite you to join by writing to us at 47 Fyfield Road, London EI7 3RE.

Notes about the contributors

Dr **David Ormrod**, lecturer in economic and social history at the University of Kent, writes on English and European commercial history in the early modern period and the social history of religion.

The Revd Canon **Stanley Evans**, canon residentiary and chancellor Southwark Cathedral 1960–1965. Founder member Christian Socialist Movement. Died 1965.

Dr **Charles Coulson**, Rouse Ball professor of mathematics at the University of Oxford 1952–1972. Vice president, Methodist conference 1959. Member of the central committee of the World Council of Churches 1962–68. Died 1974.

The Revd the Lord (Dr **Donald**) **Soper**, president, Christian Socialist Movement and its founder chair 1960–75. President Methodist conference 1953. Member of the House of Lords since 1965.

Frank Field, MP for Birkenhead since 1979, former director, Child Poverty Action Group and the Low Pay Unit.

The Revd **Kenneth Leech**, director, Runnymede Trust. Former race relations officer, Church of England Board for Social Responsibility.

Irene Brennan teaches international relations and women's studies at the Polytechnic of Central London.

The Revd **Cedric Mayson**, former staff member, Christian Institute of South Africa. Member of African National Congress, religious affairs committee.

The Revd Dr **Charles Elliott**, dean of Trinity Hall, Cambridge. Development economist. Lectured at the universities of East Anglia, Wales and Zambia. Former director of Christian Aid.

The Rt Hon **Tony Benn**, MP for Chesterfield since 1984 and Bristol South East 1950–83. Cabinet minister in Labour governments 1964–70 and 1974-79, chairman of Labour Party 1971–72.

Dr **Pauline Webb**, former organiser, religious broadcasting, BBC World Service. Vice president, Methodist conference 1965. Vice chair, central committee of the World Council of Churches 1968–75.

Peter Dawe, chair of the Christian Socialist Movement since 1983. Methodist local preacher, GLC member for Leyton 1981–86